The Gathering of Friends

Volume Six

A Year of Holidays at Home

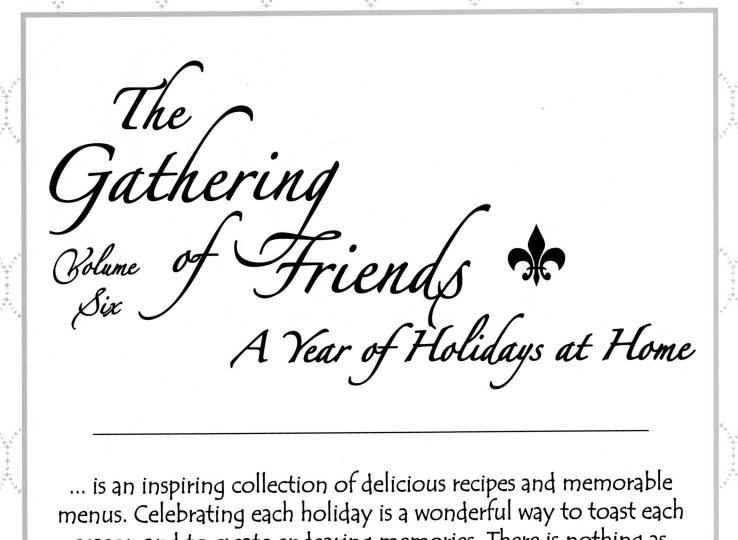

... is an inspiring collection of delicious recipes and memorable menus. Celebrating each holiday is a wonderful way to toast each season and to create endearing memories. There is nothing as magical as the anticipation of holiday celebrations. Much comfort and stability is derived from a table set with tradition.

Join us, as we celebrate *A Year of Holidays at Home*.

www.thegatheringoffriends.com

The
Gathering
of Friends ⚜

is a registered trademark of Clarenden Woods, LLC.

The Gathering of Friends
A Year of Holidays at Home
ISBN: 978-0-9816986-4-9

First Edition
10 9 8 7 6 5 4 3 2 1

Executive Editor: Michelle Huxtable
Editor in Chief: Abby Jane Green
Editor: Jean Olsen
Assistant Editor: Jocelyn Juran
Graphic Designer: Brayden Iwasaki
Photographer: Suzy O

Published by Clarenden Woods, LLC.

entertaining is...

The Gathering of Friends

a table set with grace

Dedicated to my grandchildren

⚜ Contents ⚜

⚜ Contents ⚜

Preface

Since the release of the first volume of
The Gathering of Friends, I have had thousands of
requests for a Christmas entertaining book. For this
reason, *A Year of Holidays at Home* features four
Christmas chapters with traditional flavors but new
holiday menus and inspiring ideas. We also celebrate
other seasonal favorites including, The 4th of July,
Halloween, Thanksgiving, New Year's Eve,
Valentine's and Easter.

I love my childhood memories and long for
the feelings of warmth that return as I remember my
diligent parents working tirelessly to make each holiday
special. Our celebrations revolved around the table, as
our home was always open to many who did not have a
place to celebrate. My parents generously presented
the best of what they had to share.

The way food is prepared, presented and offered up
heightens the anticipation of tasting and enjoying a
meal. This volume is filled with celebrations to bring
family and friends to the table. Our hope is to
help you savor the flavors of tradition in
A Year of Holidays at Home!

Hope & Glory

One day I met an interesting woman on a plane who shared a wonderful tradition which became the inspiration for this 4th of July celebration. She grew up on a lovely street lined with beautiful trees and colorful flower gardens where everyone took great pride in manicuring and caring for their yards.

Started by a neighborhood of patriots, this tradition brought neighbors together to celebrate American Independence in a very unusual way. Each family would bring their dining room table and chairs out onto their own front yards. At the given hour all would gather around their table and enjoy a family picnic.

As the sun went down, they would mingle and share their favorite desserts and enjoy the spirited fireworks in the night sky. Year after year this tradition became a treasured evening gathering. As children grew up and moved away, they returned home with their own families to share in this summer tradition. What a wonderful way to celebrate one of our most important holidays of the year, the fabulous Fourth!

Old Glory Fruit Tray ⚜

| 1 med. watermelon | 6 lg. firm bananas | 3 c. fresh blueberries |

Cut watermelon into small bite-size pieces. Peel and slice bananas. Rinse fresh blueberries and pat dry. Design fruit flag on an oblong serving tray by placing blueberries in upper left corner. Arrange watermelon and bananas to form red and white stripes (as pictured).

B.L.T. Slaw ⚜

1 ½ lbs. precooked bacon
1 ½ c. cherry tomatoes

1 head green cabbage
½ head iceberg lettuce

½ c. flat Italian parsley

Preheat oven to 400°. With scissors, snip bacon and place on a jelly roll pan. Bake in oven for 3 to 4 minutes or until crisp. Set aside to cool.

Rinse tomatoes and slice into small circles. Shred cabbage and chop lettuce; rinse and pat dry. Clean, dry and chop parsley. Combine all ingredients in a bowl and toss with Creamy Garlic Pepper Dressing. Chill.

Creamy Garlic Pepper Dressing ⚜

½ c. mayonnaise
½ c. rice vinegar
½ tsp. kosher salt
½ tsp. coarse black pepper
⅓ c. sugar
1 tsp. garlic pepper

Whisk all ingredients together and chill before serving.

Corn Nibbles ⚜

8 ears fresh corn
¼ c. mayonnaise
⅓ c. grated Parmesan cheese
½ tsp. parsley flakes
4 limes
1 tsp. ground cumin

Bring a large pot of water to a boil. Cut corn on the cob into chunks, (as pictured). Boil corn for 3 to 4 minutes; remove from water and place corn in a large Ziploc™ bag. In a small bowl, stir together mayonnaise, Parmesan cheese and parsley flakes. Add Parmesan mixture to corn. Drizzle lime juice on corn. Seal bag and toss evenly. Sprinkle with cumin and season to taste. Place in bowl and serve.

Creamy Italian Dressing ⚜

½ c. vegetable oil
1 c. plain yogurt
½ c. sugar

½ c. apple cider vinegar
½ tsp. coarse black pepper

½ tsp. onion salt
½ tsp. garlic salt

Combine all ingredients together in a blender and mix well. Serve with Star Studded Pasta Salad.

Star Studded Pasta Salad ⚜

1 lb. fresh three cheese tortellini
1 ½ lbs. sliced deli salami
3 sm. cucumbers

6 celery stalks
½ c. flat Italian parsley

1 16 oz. jar baby corn on the cob
3 lg. red bell peppers

Cook cheese tortellini al dente, according to directions on package; rinse and chill. Slice salami into long strips. Clean and dice cucumbers into small pieces. Chop celery and parsley. Chop baby corn into small bite-size pieces. Cut red peppers in half and remove seeds: lay flat on a chopping board. Using a small star cookie cutter, cut red peppers into small star shapes. Set 10 stars aside to garnish the top of the salad. In a large serving bowl, toss all ingredients together and add Creamy Italian Dressing. Garnish with bell pepper stars. Cover and chill until ready to serve.

Potato Stacks ⚜

6 lg. russet potatoes
2 tbsp. olive oil
1 tsp. kosher salt
cilantro, garnish

Preheat oven to 375°. Clean and slice large potatoes into wide, ½-inch thick slices (as pictured). Brush with olive oil and season with kosher salt; place potato slices on a jelly roll pan.

Bake for 30 to 40 minutes, turning twice until fully cooked, but firm. Place on serving tray and top with Picnic Pulled Pork. Garnish with a sprig of cilantro. Serve immediately.

Picnic Pulled Pork ⚜

4 ½ lbs. pork tenderloin

1 c. Coke™

Seasoned Pork Rub:
3 tbsp. brown sugar
2 tsp. kosher salt
1 tsp. coarse black pepper
1 ½ tsp. ground paprika
½ tsp. dried mustard

½ tsp. onion powder
¼ tsp. garlic powder
¼ tsp. garlic salt
¼ tsp. celery salt

¾ tsp. ground cinnamon
¼ tsp. ground ginger
¼ tsp. ground nutmeg
1 tbsp. parsley flakes

Sweet Pork Sauce:
 - ⅓ c. balsamic vinegar
 - ⅓ c. honey
 - 1 ½ c. Coke™
 - ½ c. brown sugar
 - olive oil for browning

Cut pork tenderloin into large chunks. Pour Coke™ into a Ziploc™ bag and add pork. Marinate for at least 2 hours.

Mix all spices together in a bowl and blend well. Remove pork from refrigerator and drain Coke™ from bag. Cover each piece of pork with Seasoned Pork Rub and return to bag. Refrigerate 2 more hours or overnight.

In a small bowl, mix together vinegar, honey, Coke™ and brown sugar. Set aside sauce.

Heat olive oil in a heavy pot and brown the marinated pork on all sides. Slow cook pork, adding Sweet Pork Sauce to pot or slow cooker; cooking time will depend on whether using a pot on the stove (2 to 4 hours over medium-low heat) or a slow cooker (4 to 6 hours on high). Pull pork apart with forks. Serve over Potato Stacks.

Helpful Hint: This recipe can also be used in pulled pork sandwiches, burritos or a salad.

Barbecue Baked Beans ⚜

1 c. barbecue sauce

¾ c. brown sugar

3 tbsp. Dijon mustard

¼ c. apple cider vinegar

2 tbsp. olive oil

1 green bell pepper

1 red bell pepper

1 white onion

¾ lb. sliced deli ham

3 15 oz. cans pork and beans

1 15 oz. can Great Northern beans

Preheat oven to 325°. In a small mixing bowl, combine barbecue sauce, brown sugar, mustard and vinegar. Set aside. Heat olive oil in a large skillet over medium heat. Clean, seed and dice bell peppers, peel and dice onion. Place in skillet with hot olive oil. Dice ham and add to skillet. Stirring occasionally, cook until peppers and onions are tender, 2 to 4 minutes. Stir in pork and beans and Great Northern beans. Pour in the barbecue sauce mixture and bring to a simmer for about 5 minutes. Transfer to a large baking dish and bake for 2 hours.

Sugar Star Cookies ⚜

½ c. butter, softened
½ c. shortening
½ c. sugar
½ c. powdered sugar

1 egg, whisked
1 tsp. pure vanilla extract
2 ¼ c. flour

½ tsp. cream of tartar
½ tsp. kosher salt
½ tsp. baking soda

Preheat oven to 350°. In a mixing bowl blend butter, shortening and both sugars together, until creamy. Fold in egg and vanilla.

In a separate bowl, whisk all dry ingredients together. Combine with butter mixture and blend well. Roll dough out ¼ to ½-inch thick and cut into stars using a star shaped cookie cutter, or desired shape. Place on jelly roll pan sprayed with cooking spray. Bake for 6 to 8 minutes. Place on cookie rack to cool.

Butter Cream Frosting ⚜

6 oz. cream cheese
1 c. butter, softened
2 tsp. pure vanilla extract
4 c. powdered sugar
1 c. sliced strawberries, garnish
½ c. fresh blackberries, garnish

Place cream cheese and butter in a bowl. Using an electric mixer beat for 2 to 3 minutes. Add vanilla and powdered sugar. Whip until light and fluffy. Rinse and dry berries. Frost cookies and top with strawberries and blackberries (as pictured).

Lemon Blueberry Pound Cake ⚜

1 ½ c. flour
1 tsp. baking powder
¼ tsp. kosher salt
1 tbsp. lemon zest

1 c. fresh blueberries, rinsed
½ c. butter, softened
¾ c. sugar

2 eggs
1 tsp. pure vanilla extract
½ c. milk

Preheat oven to 350°. Prepare a loaf pan with cooking spray. In a medium-size mixing bowl, combine whisk flour, baking powder, salt and lemon zest. Remove 1 tablespoon of the flour mixture to coat blueberries. In another bowl, toss blueberries with the flour mixture and set aside.

In a separate bowl, with an electric mixer, beat the butter and sugar together until creamy. Fold in eggs and vanilla until combined. Add dry ingredients and milk to butter mixture. Mix only until combined. Gently fold in coated blueberries.

Place batter in an 8 x 4 loaf pan and bake for 55 to 65 minutes or until cake is golden and toothpick inserted in the center comes out clean.

Lemon Glaze ⚜

²/₃ c. powdered sugar
zest of 1 lemon
1 tbsp. fresh lemon juice

Stir sugar, zest and lemon juice in a small bowl and blend well. Pour over cooled cake and serve.

Details...

All American, All Delicious! This simply delicious combination of all American favorites is perfect for any gathering.

Details...

Fill a large crock with ice and chill pop bottles with attached flag stickers. For a touch of patriotism just add Old Glory!

Details...

This colonial style home is the perfect setting for a patriotic 4th of July celebration.

As a clever candleholder, we chose to use a colander, with a large white candle filled with cheerful green parsley.

Shopping List

Each recipe is designed to serve eight to ten

¾ lb. sliced deli ham
4 ½ lbs. pork tenderloin
1 ½ lbs. sliced deli salami
1 ½ lbs. precooked bacon
1 c. plain yogurt
6 oz. cream cheese
⅓ c. grated Parmesan cheese
1 green bell pepper
4 lg. red bell peppers
1 white onion
6 lg. russet potatoes
3 sm. cucumbers
6 celery stalks
1 bunch flat Italian parsley
1 bunch cilantro
1 ½ c. cherry tomatoes

1 head green cabbage
½ head iceberg lettuce
8 ears fresh corn
4 limes
2 lemons
1 med. watermelon
6 lg. firm bananas
4 c. fresh blueberries
1 c. fresh strawberries
1 c. fresh blackberries
1 ½ tsp. ground paprika
½ tsp. dried mustard
½ tsp. onion powder
¼ tsp. garlic powder
¼ tsp. celery salt
3 ½ tsp. parsley flakes

Shopping List

Each recipe is designed to serve eight to ten

1 tsp. garlic pepper
1 tsp. ground cumin
½ tsp. cream of tartar
1 lb. fresh three cheese tortellini
1 c. barbecue sauce
⅓ c. balsamic vinegar
¾ c. apple cider vinegar

½ c. rice vinegar
3 tbsp. Dijon mustard
1 16 oz. jar baby corn on the cob
3 15 oz. cans pork and beans
1 15 oz. can Great Northern beans
2 12 oz. cans Coke™

Staples:

flour
baking powder
baking soda
ground cinnamon
ground ginger
ground nutmeg
pure vanilla extract
sugar

powdered sugar
brown sugar
milk
eggs
butter
shortening
vegetable oil
olive oil

honey
kosher salt
garlic salt
onion salt
coarse black pepper
mayonnaise

shopping lists available for print online.

-CHAPTER TWO-

Fun & Fright

Enter if you dare... and enjoy this slightly spooky menu of deliciously deranged dishes for Halloween that will bewitch your family and friends. With a chill in the air and a nip of frost, this eerie evening will bring ghosts and goblins to your door.

Even the shadows in the dark will want to join in the ghoulish fun and gather around a grinning tabletop Jack-o'-lantern. A mixture of frightfully festive recipes include Monster Mash Gauc & Chips, Mini Mummies, Wicked Good Mac & Cheese, comforting lasagna with an autumn glow, Little Cheese Critters, Black Widows, caramel apple orchard ghosts and a variety of tempting treats.

The flickering candles warn us to beware of what lurks within this autumn feast. It may be scary and silly but oh… so much fun!

Orange Shrimp Pasta Salad ⚜

10 oz. pkg. bow tie pasta
1 c. pumpkin seeds, toasted
1 lb. shrimp, cooked, deveined
2   11 oz. cans mandarin oranges
3 c. arugula leaves

Preheat oven to 375°. Cook pasta al dente, according to instructions on package. Drain and set aside.

Spread pumpkin seeds on jelly roll pan and roast in oven for 10 to 12 minutes. Remove from oven and cool.

Rinse shrimp. Remove and discard tails. Drain mandarin oranges. Toss pasta, pumpkin seeds, shrimp, mandarin oranges and arugula together in a bowl. Top with Black Poppy Seed Salad Dressing just before serving.

Black Poppy Seed Dressing ⚜

2 limes, juice
½ c. vegetable oil
1 tsp. poppy seeds

¾ c. sugar
½ tsp. kosher salt

Slice limes in half and juice; whisk lime juice and oil together. Add poppy seeds, sugar and salt; blend well. Chill before serving.

Monster Mash Guac & Chips ⚜

2 ripe avocados
½ red onion
2 tbsp. cilantro
1 lime, juice
½ tsp. kosher salt
½ tsp. coarse black pepper
1 jalapeno pepper
1 sm. zucchini, cored and minced
1 11 oz. pkg. blue corn tortilla chips

Cut avocados in half. Remove pit. Scoop out avocado from the peel and place in mixing bowl. Using a fork, roughly mash the avocado. Peel and dice onion and finely chop cilantro. Slice lime in half and squeeze juice over avocado. Add onion, cilantro, salt and pepper.

Remove stem and dice half of jalapeno pepper with seeds. Fold into guacamole. Add remaining diced jalapeno with or without seeds depending on desired heat. Core and finely mince zucchini and fold into Monster Mash Guac.

Cover with plastic wrap directly on the surface of the guacamole to prevent oxidation from the air. Refrigerate. Serve with blue corn tortilla chips (as pictured).

Mini Mummies ⚜

1 8 oz. can crescent rolls
1 13 oz. pkg. beef sausage Lit'l Smokies™
3 tbsp. butter, melted
½ tsp. garlic salt

Preheat oven to 375°. Open crescent rolls and spread out on flat surface. Cut in ½-inch strips no longer than 1 ½-inches long. Wrap and stretch a strip of dough around each smokie and place on a jelly roll pan.

Bake for 10 to 12 minutes or until golden brown. Remove from oven and brush with melted butter and season with garlic salt.

Easy BBQ Dipping Sauce ⚜

¾ c. brown sugar
¾ c. ketchup
¼ c. red wine vinegar
¼ c. water
1 tbsp. Worcestershire sauce

1 ¼ tsp. ground mustard
1 tsp. paprika
¾ tsp. kosher salt
½ tsp. coarse black pepper

Place all ingredients in a mixing bowl. Whisk until the sugar has dissolved and the spices are well blended. Serve immediately or cover and store in refrigerator. Serve with *Mini Mummies*.

Wicked Good Mac & Cheese ⚜

1 tbsp. olive oil
1 tsp. kosher salt
1 lb. pkg. macaroni
½ c. butter
⅓ c. flour
2 tsp. granulated chicken bouillon
½ tsp. kosher salt
1 tsp. coarse black pepper
3 c. milk
3 c. grated sharp cheddar cheese
2 green onions, garnish

In a large stockpot, bring water to a boil and add olive oil and salt; stir in macaroni. Cook according to directions on package. Drain, rinse and set aside.

Preheat oven to 375°. Melt butter in a medium-size pot and whisk in flour, bouillon, salt and pepper. Slowly whisk in milk. Cook for 2 to 3 minutes. Fold in cheese and blend until smooth. Pour over cooked macaroni and stir to evenly coat.

Place in individual containers or a 9 x 13 pan prepared with cooking spray and bake for 45 minutes or until cheese begins to brown around the edges. Bake smaller servings for less time; watch for cheese to crisp around the edges. Garnish with diced green onions when ready to serve.

Cauldron Baked Lasagna ⚜

1 lb. pkg. lasagna noodles
3 c. heavy whipping cream
1 c. grated Parmesan cheese
2 cloves garlic
1 tsp. kosher salt
1 white onion
1 red bell pepper
2 lg. carrots
1 c. fresh green beans
1 c. frozen white corn
6-8 acorn squash (optional for baking)
2 c. shredded mozzarella cheese
4 Roma tomatoes
1 tbsp. sugar
½ tsp. coarse black pepper
4 green onions, garnish

This recipe makes lasagna for a 9 x 13 baking dish or 6 to 8 individual servings of lasagna baked in acorn squash.

Prepare lasagna noodles according to directions on package; drain and set aside. Preheat oven to 375°. In a large stockpot, heat cream to a simmer. Add Parmesan cheese and continue to simmer. Cook for 2 to 3 more minutes; remove from heat, mince garlic and add garlic and salt to cream sauce.

Peel and chop onion. Seed and dice bell pepper. Peel and thinly slice carrots. Slice green beans into small pieces. Keep each vegetable separated for preparing lasagna layers. If baking in acorn squash, slice off tops and remove seeds and stringy pulp from each squash and discard.

Spread a thin layer of cream sauce in the bottom of a baking dish or in bottom of the acorn squash. Place a layer of noodles, onions and frozen corn; top with sauce and mozzarella cheese. Add 2nd layer of noodles, topped with bell peppers, cream sauce and cheese. Add 3rd layer of noodles, carrots and green beans, cream sauce and cheese. Finish with a layer of noodles and top with cream sauce and cheese.

Rinse and slice tomatoes, and place as the top layer, then sprinkle with sugar and pepper. Replace lid and line a 9 x 13 baking dish with acorn squash. Bake for 30 to 35 minutes. Slice green onions and garnish. Serve.

placemats and napkins available at thegatheringoffriends.com

Little Cheese Critters ⚜

1 8 oz. pkg. cream cheese, softened
1 tsp. garlic pepper
1 c. grated sharp cheddar cheese, divided

½ c. chow mein noodles
2 drops black paste food coloring

Set aside 1 teaspoon of cream cheese to mix with black paste food coloring for garnish. In a small mixing bowl combine cream cheese, garlic pepper, and 2 tablespoons cheddar cheese. Form small ½-inch cheese balls and roll in remaining cheddar cheese.

Place 4 noodles as spider legs on each side of the cheese balls. Mix black paste food coloring with remaining teaspoon of cream cheese in plastic bag and clip one corner; apply small eyes on each cheese ball (as pictured). Cover and chill until ready to serve.

Witch's Chili Brew ⚜

1 white onion
1 ½ lbs. ground turkey
1 ½ tsp. kosher salt
1 tsp. coarse black pepper
2 15 oz. cans tomato sauce

1 14.5 oz. can diced tomatoes
3 1.25 oz. pkgs. chili seasoning mix
½ c. brown sugar
3 16 oz. cans kidney beans

1–2 c. water
12 bread bowls
½ c. cilantro, chopped
Little Cheese Critters

Peel and dice onion. In a large stockpot over medium heat, sauté ground turkey with diced white onion, salt and pepper. Stir occasionally until meat is brown and completely cooked. Stir in tomato sauce, diced tomatoes, chili seasoning and brown sugar. Drain and rinse kidney beans and add to chili. Cook until completely heated, stirring to keep bottom from burning. Add 1 to 2 cups water, as desired.

Prepare bread bowls by slicing off tops and removing the center bread, leaving about a ½-inch thick shell.

When ready to serve, fill bread bowls with chili and garnish with Little Cheese Critters and cilantro.

Little Cheese Critters will melt in hot chili.

Black Widows ⚜

1 ½ c. semisweet chocolate chips, divided
2 c. sweetened flake coconut

¼ c. chow mein noodles
10 pieces Swedish Fish™

Line a jelly roll pan with parchment paper. Melt 1 ¼ cups chocolate chips in a glass bowl in the microwave. Heat for 20 seconds at a time, stirring between, until completely melted. Do not overcook. Stir coconut gently into melted chocolate. As chocolate begins to cool, take a heaping spoonful and lightly roll into a ball. Place balls side by side on a parchment-lined jelly roll pan.

Melt remaining chocolate chips. Add chow mein noodles to melted chocolate. Carefully take chocolate-coated noodles and place as legs on the sides of each coconut spider. Cut off the end tips of the tails of the candy fish and add red eyes to each spider. Place on serving tray and chill.

Halloween Delight Kettle Corn ⚜

1 18 oz. bag popped kettle corn

1 12 oz. pkg. white chocolate chips

1 12 oz. pkg. mini semisweet chocolate chips

12 orange slice candies

Place kettle corn in a large mixing bowl. Melt white chocolate chips in a glass bowl in the microwave. Heat for 20 seconds at a time, stirring between, until completely melted. Do not overcook. Fold melted chocolate into the kettle corn and stir until completely coated. Gently toss kettle corn with mini chocolate chips and spread out on 2 jelly roll pans. Cut orange slices into small pieces with scissors and sprinkle over warm popcorn. Chill in refrigerator for 15 minutes. Break into pieces and place in a serving bowl.

Pumpkin Cream Cheese Squares ⚜

3 eggs, divided
2 c. + 1 tbsp. sugar, divided
½ c. vegetable oil
1 c. canned pumpkin

2 ¼ c. flour
1 tbsp. pumpkin pie spice
1 tsp. baking soda

½ tsp. kosher salt
½ tsp. pure vanilla extract
8 oz. pkg. cream cheese, softened

Preheat oven to 350°. Combine 2 eggs, 2 cups sugar, oil and pumpkin in a mixing bowl and beat together. In a separate bowl, combine flour, pumpkin pie spice, baking soda and salt. Add dry ingredients to pumpkin mixture; mix well and pour into a greased 9-inch square baking dish.

Combine remaining egg, 1 tablespoon sugar, vanilla and cream cheese in a small mixing bowl. Beat with an electric mixer. Spoon cream cheese batter over pumpkin batter in baking dish and swirl with knife. Bake for 35 to 45 minutes or until a toothpick inserted in center comes out clean. Chill and cut into squares. Serve.

Autumn Ice Cream Pie

½ c. butter

2 c. Anna's Ginger Thins™, crushed

1 ¾ qts. vanilla ice cream, softened

1 ¾ c. sugar

1 tsp. ground cinnamon

¾ tsp. ground ginger

¾ tsp. ground nutmeg

½ tsp. kosher salt

2 c. canned pumpkin

1 c. heavy whipping cream

1 can dairy whipped topping, garnish

nutmeg, garnish

Melt butter and combine with cookie crumbs. Press into a 9 x 13 airtight container. Freeze crust.

Soften ice cream at room temperature for about 5 minutes. Spread the slightly softened ice cream evenly over the frozen crust.

In a bowl, whisk sugar, spices and salt; stir in pumpkin. Whip cream to firm peaks and fold into pumpkin-spice mixture until well combined. Evenly Spoon the pumpkin topping over the softened ice cream. Cover and freeze until firm.

Remove pumpkin dessert from the freezer 5 minutes before serving. Cut into squares. Garnish with whipped cream and a sprinkle of nutmeg.

Ghosts of Halloween Past ⚜

10 Granny Smith apples

Caramel:

½ c. butter

2 c. brown sugar

1 c. light corn syrup

1 14 oz. can sweetened condensed milk

1 tsp. pure vanilla extract

5 4 oz. Ghirardelli™ white chocolate baking bars

Black Cows™ or black licorice jelly beans

Wash and dry apples and set aside. In a stockpot combine butter, brown sugar and corn syrup, stirring constantly. Bring to a boil over medium heat. Lower heat and add condensed milk. Continue to stir as caramel mixture simmers. When a drizzle of hot caramel is dropped into a small cup of water and forms a firm ball, remove from heat. Stir in vanilla and allow to slightly cool before dipping apples.

Instead of wooden sticks, place cutting knives inside apple cores. Dip each apple in slightly cooled caramel and place on a serving tray to cool and harden.

Melt chocolate in a glass bowl in the microwave. Heat for 20 seconds at a time, stirring between, until completely melted. Do not overcook. Pour white chocolate over caramel apples spreading evenly with a spatula (as pictured). Make eyes by cutting Black Cows™ or jelly beans into slices and placing on each caramel apple ghost. *Use knives responsibly.*

Goblin Bars

¾ c. butter
½ c. sugar
4 c. graham cracker crumbs

1 14 oz. can sweetened condensed milk
1 12 oz. pkg. semisweet chocolate chips
1 12 oz. pkg. peanut butter chips

Preheat oven to 350°. Melt butter in a mixing bowl and fold in sugar and graham cracker crumbs; mix well. Place crumb mixture in a 9 x 13 baking pan and gently press down to make crust.

Cover crust evenly with condensed milk. Sprinkle chocolate and peanut butter chips over the top. Bake for 20 to 25 minutes or until golden brown on edges. Let cool and cut into small squares to serve.

placemats and napkins available at thegatheringoffriends.com.

Details...

These Little Cheese Critters are melt-in-your-mouth good! As they creep into the hot chili bread bowls, they will add a cheesy, creamy flavor sure to please all the goblins at your table.

Notes & Comments

_____
_____
_____
_____
_____
_____
_____
_____
_____
_____
_____
_____
_____
_____
_____
_____

Shopping List

Each recipe is designed to serve ten to twelve

1½ lbs. ground turkey
13 oz. pkg. beef sausage Lit'l Smokies™
1 lb. shrimp, cooked, deveined
4 c. grated sharp cheddar cheese
1 c. grated Parmesan cheese
2 c. shredded mozzarella cheese
4 c. heavy whipping cream
2 8 oz. pkgs. cream cheese
2 11 oz. cans mandarin oranges
1 ¾ qts. vanilla ice cream
1 can dairy whipped topping
1 8 oz. can crescent rolls
2 white onions
½ red onion
6 green onions
1 red bell pepper
2 lg. carrots
1 c. fresh green beans
6-8 acorn squash
1 bunch cilantro

2 cloves garlic
4 Roma tomatoes
1 c. pumpkin seeds
3 c. arugula leaves
3 limes
2 ripe avocados
1 jalapeno pepper
1 sm. zucchini
1 c. frozen white corn
10 Granny Smith apples
3 1.25 oz. pkgs. chili seasoning mix
2 tsp. granulated chicken bouillon
1 tsp. garlic pepper
1 ¼ tsp. ground mustard
1 tsp. paprika
1 tsp. poppy seeds
1 tbsp. pumpkin pie spice
1 lb. pkg. macaroni
1 lb. pkg. lasagna noodles
10 oz. pkg. bow tie pasta

-CHAPTER TWO-

Shopping List

Each recipe is designed to serve ten to twelve

¾ c. chow mein noodles
12 bread bowls
¼ c. red wine vinegar
2 15 oz. cans tomato sauce
1 14.5 oz. can diced tomatoes
3 16 oz. cans kidney beans
3 c. canned pumpkin
2 14 oz. can sweetened condensed milk
1 18 oz. bag popped kettle corn
1 12 oz. pkg. white chocolate chips
1 12 oz. pkg. mini semisweet chocolate chips

2 12 oz. pkg. semisweet chocolate chips
1 12 oz. pkg. peanut butter chips
5 4 oz. Ghirardelli™ white chocolate baking bars
2 c. sweetened flake coconut
4 c. graham cracker crumbs
2 c. Anna's Ginger Thins™, crushed
10 pieces Swedish Fish™
12 orange slice candies
Black Cows™ or black licorice jelly beans
black paste food coloring
1 11 oz. pkg blue corn tortilla chips

Staples:

flour
baking soda
ground cinnamon
ground ginger
ground nutmeg
pure vanilla extract
sugar

brown sugar
milk
eggs
butter
vegetable oil
olive oil
light corn syrup

kosher salt
garlic salt
coarse black pepper
granulated chicken bouillon
Worcestershire sauce
ketchup

shopping lists available for print online.

-CHAPTER THREE-

Bountifully Blessed

Thanksgiving ushers in the winter holiday
season, as thankful hearts join together to reflect
and give thanks. Celebrate abundance with this
feast without the fuss. Simple Bacon Wrapped
Turkey Tenderloins, oven roasted in less than an
hour, plentiful side dishes and familiar sweets
complement these flavors worth savoring.

This is a time to give praise as everyone is
together again around a welcoming table.
Grateful hearts enjoy these delicious holiday
pleasures. Our special new recipes will fill your
season of thanks with memories
to honor tradition.

Divine Dinner Rolls ⚜

- 1 4 oz. pkg. active dry yeast
- 1 c. warm water
- ¼ c. honey
- 1 tsp. kosher salt
- 1 egg, whisked
- 3 c. flour
- 1 tbsp. butter, melted
- 1 tsp. parsley flakes
- ½ tsp. kosher salt

In a mixing bowl, combine yeast and warm water; let sit for 5 minutes, until bubbly. Add honey, salt and egg. Stir until well blended. Add flour and mix with a wooden spoon until dough comes together. Knead the dough on a lightly floured surface until soft and elastic, about 6 to 8 minutes, adding more flour if the dough is too sticky. Do not add too much flour; the dough will become more workable the longer you knead it.

Place kneaded dough in a lightly oiled bowl and cover with plastic wrap. Let rise in a warm area until dough has doubled in size, about 2 hours. Punch down dough and divide into small balls, the size of golf balls; place on a jelly roll pan 2 inches apart. Cover with a kitchen towel and let rise for 20 minutes.

Preheat oven to 400°. Brush rolls with melted butter and sprinkle with parsley flakes and salt. Bake for 10 to 12 minutes.

Spiced Cranberry Wreath ⚜

2 6 oz. pkg. raspberry Jell-O™
3 c. boiling water
2 14 oz. cans whole berry cranberry sauce
2 tart apples
1 ½ c. walnuts, chopped

1 20 oz. can crushed pineapple
½ c. sugar
¼ tsp. ground cloves
½ tsp. ground nutmeg
1 bunch flat Italian parsley, garnish

Add Jell-O™ into boiling water and stir until completely dissolved. Pour into a mixing bowl and fold in cranberry sauce; stir until dissolved. Peel, core and dice apples. Chop walnuts. Add apples, walnut, pineapple, sugar and spices to bowl of Jell-O™ and mix well. Pour jelled mixture into 2 small bundt pans and chill in refrigerator, until firm, at least 2 hours or overnight. Remove from molds and place rings on plate stands. Garnish with fresh parsley stems to complete the wreath.

Sourdough Sausage Dressing ⚜

1 lb. loaf sour dough bread
6 tbsp. olive oil, divided
1 ½ tsp. kosher salt, divided
1 lg. yellow onion
1 ½ c. diced celery
2 cloves garlic
1 bundle asparagus
1 lb. button mushrooms
1 lb. spicy Italian ground sausage
1 ½ tsp. Italian seasoning
1 ½ tsp. poultry seasoning
1 tsp. dried rosemary
½ tsp. coarse black pepper
1 ½ c. chicken broth
1 egg, whisked
1 c. grated Parmesan cheese

Preheat oven to 375°. Cut bread slices into cubes and toss with 4 tbsp. olive oil and 1 teaspoon salt. Spread evenly on a jelly roll pan and bake until golden brown and crusty, about 12 to 15 minutes. Peel and dice onion and rinse and dice celery. Peel and mince garlic. Cut off bottom 2 inches of asparagus and discard. Rinse and chop spears into 2-inch pieces. Clean and slice mushrooms.

In a large pot, cook sausage, stirring until fully cooked. Remove from pot and set aside in a bowl. In the same pot, add remaining 2 tbsp. olive oil and sauté asparagus, onion, celery, garlic and mushrooms. Cook for 2 minutes.

Whisk all seasonings and remaining ½ tsp. salt together in a large bowl. Add chicken broth, beaten egg and sausage. Fold in toasted bread cubes, Parmesan cheese and sautéed vegetables. Place dressing in a buttered 9 x 13 pan. Cover and bake for 30 minutes; remove foil and bake an additional 10 minutes.

Baked Sweet Yams ⚜

5 lg. yams
3 c. water
4 tbsp. butter
2 ¼ c. brown sugar

¾ tsp. ground cinnamon
¼ tsp. ground nutmeg
1 10 oz. pkg. miniature marshmallows

Preheat oven to 400°. Wash and dry the yams; bake for 1 hour or until soft. While yams are baking, combine water, butter, brown sugar, and spices in a saucepan. Bring the butter and brown sugar mixture to a boil in saucepan; reduce heat and simmer for 30 to 45 minutes or until sauce thickens.
Remove yams from oven and let cool; peel. Reduce oven temperature to 350°.

Slice potatoes into ½-inch cubes and place in a casserole dish. Pour syrup over yams and cover the top with marshmallows. Return to oven and bake for approximately 30 minutes.

candles by Vance Kitira

Green Beans & Carrots in Garlic Pepper ⚜

8 lg. carrots	4 tbsp. butter
3 c. slim green beans	2 tsp. garlic pepper

Peel large carrots and cut in large diagonal pieces (as pictured). Snip ends of green beans and rinse. Bring water to a boil in a large stockpot. Place carrots in first and cook for 1 to 2 minutes. Add green beans and cook for 3 more minutes or until desired tenderness. Rinse in colander and return to pot. Toss with butter and garlic pepper; place in serving bowl.

Turkey Gravy ⚜

turkey drippings from the tenderloins
3 tbsp. butter

¼ c. flour
2-3 c. chicken or turkey broth

Place turkey drippings in large stockpot over medium heat. Add butter and melt. Whisk in flour to create a roux, whisk until crumbly. Continue to cook until the roux is a dark brown color and fragrant. Add the stock to the roux and whisk to combine. Turn heat to high and bring liquid to a boil while still stirring. Once the liquid reaches a boil, reduce heat and simmer. Stir until gravy thickens.

Helpful Hint: To create more gravy, add 1 package of turkey gravy mix and 1 cup of water, simmer. Serve with White Cheddar Mashed Potatoes.

White Cheddar Mashed Potatoes ⚜

5 lbs. russet potatoes
½ c. butter
1 ½ tsp. kosher salt
1 tsp. coarse black pepper
½-1 c. milk or heavy whipping cream
2 c. shredded white cheddar cheese

Clean and peel potatoes; cut into large chunks. Place in a large stockpot and cover with water. Boil for 15 to 20 minutes or until tender. Drain water. Add butter, salt, pepper, cream and cheese. Mash to desired consistency and serve.

Bacon Wrapped Turkey Tenderloins ⚜

| olive oil | 1 tsp. garlic pepper | 2 lbs. bacon slices |
| 2 tsp. dried rosemary | 6 1 lb. turkey tenderloins | |

Preheat oven to 325°. In a large stockpot, heat olive oil, rosemary and garlic pepper on high. Sear turkey tenderloins on all sides to seal in the natural juices and place on a jelly roll pan. Set stockpot aside to make Turkey Gravy after tenderloins are cooked.

Wrap 3 or 4 slices of bacon under the turkey tenderloins and tie on top (as pictured). Bake tenderloins until thermometer inserted near center registers 160°, approximately 45 minutes.

Apple Orchard Crisp ⚜

7 tart apples
2 lemons

¾ c. flour
1 ½ c. sugar

1 ½ tsp. ground cinnamon
½ c. cold butter

Crumble Topping:
1 ½ c. brown sugar
1 tsp. ground cinnamon

½ tsp. kosher salt
2 c. rolled oats

¾ c. flour
½ c. butter, softened

Preheat oven to 400°. Peel, core and slice apples. Slice lemons in half and squeeze juice of both lemons over apples. Whisk flour, sugar and cinnamon together and toss over apple slices. Place apple mixture in buttered baking dish. Cut butter into slices and place evenly over apples.

In a mixing bowl, combine brown sugar, cinnamon, salt, oats and flour. Cut in butter and blend until mixture is crumbly. Sprinkle crumble on top of the sweetened apple slices. Bake for 30 minutes.

Thanksgiving Pecan Pie ⚜

candles by Vance Kitira

Pastry:
- 1 ½ c. flour
- ½ tsp. kosher salt
- ½ c. shortening
- 5 tbsp. ice water

Pecan Filling:
- 1 c. light corn syrup
- 1 c. sugar
- 3 eggs, whisked
- 2 tbsp. butter, melted
- 1 tsp. pure vanilla extract
- 1 ½ c. pecan halves

Preheat oven to 350°. Whisk flour and salt together. Cut in shortening with pastry blender to form small pea-size pieces. Sprinkle with ice water and combine with hands to form a soft ball of dough; handle as little as possible.

Place ball of dough on floured surface. Roll softly with a floured rolling pin, from the center outward in each direction, to form a flat circle of dough. Fold dough in half and place in pie dish. Over hang the pastry and cut edges with a knife to remove excess dough. Pinch edges to form a pretty crust. In a medium mixing bowl, mix corn syrup, sugar, eggs, butter and vanilla; mix with a spoon. Stir in pecans and pour filling into pie crust. Bake pie on center rack of oven for 60 to 70 minutes or until the filling is cooked in the center.

Helpful Hint: If you are in a hurry use an unbaked or frozen deep-dish pie crust.

Spiced Pumpkin Cake ⚜

4 eggs
1 ²/₃ c. sugar
1 c. vegetable oil
1 29 oz. can canned pumpkin

2 c. flour
2 tsp. baking powder
1 tsp. baking soda

1 tsp. kosher salt
1 tsp. ground cinnamon
½ tsp. ground cloves

Preheat oven to 350°. Combine eggs, sugar, oil and pumpkin in a large mixing bowl and blend with an electric mixer.

In a separate bowl, combine remaining dry ingredients and whisk together. Add dry ingredients to pumpkin mixture. Beat for 3 to 4 minutes on medium speed. Pour into 3 greased 9-inch round cake pans.

Bake for 20 to 25 minutes or until toothpick inserted in the center of the cakes comes out clean. Remove from baking pans and wrap immediately in plastic wrap and allow to completely cool.

Once cooled, place one of the cakes on a cake stand and frost first layer with Almond Cream Cheese Frosting. Add second layer and repeat. Finish with third layer and frost entire cake evenly. Refrigerate until ready to serve.

Almond Cream Cheese Frosting ⚜

4 oz. cream cheese, softened	1 tbsp. heavy whipping cream	1 tsp. almond extract
½ c. butter, softened	4 c. powdered sugar	½ tsp. pure vanilla extract

Combine ingredients together with an electric mixer in a small mixing bowl and beat until creamy. Frost Spiced Pumpkin Cake.

candles by Vance Kitira - vancekitira.com

Details...

Festive pear themed candles placed on autumn colored ceramic leaf-shaped dishes light this tablescape.

For a special Thanksgiving touch, add a turkey-shaped butter mold to accent this tablescape.

Details...

A grand scale hurricane candle stands proudly surrounded by harvest pears at the center of this gracious tablescape.

Charming holiday fruit and nut filled wreaths entwined with branches of acorns accent these subtle colors to creatively dress this harvest table.

Shopping List

Each recipe is designed to serve twelve plus

6 1 lb. turkey tenderloins
2 lbs. bacon slices
1 lb. spicy Italian ground sausage
2 c. shredded white cheddar cheese
1 c. grated Parmesan cheese
1 c. heavy whipping cream
2 lbs. butter
1 4 oz. cream cheese
8 lg. carrots
3 c. slim green beans
5 lbs. russet potatoes
5 lg. yams
1 lb. button mushrooms

1 lg. yellow onion
1 head celery
2 cloves garlic
1 bundle asparagus
9 tart apples
2 lemons
1 bunch flat Italian parsley
1 tsp. parsley flakes
3 tsp. garlic pepper
3 tsp. dried rosemary
1 ½ tsp. Italian seasoning
1 ½ tsp. poultry seasoning
¾ tsp. ground cloves

Shopping List

Each recipe is designed to serve twelve plus

1 tsp. almond extract
1 4 oz. pkg. active dry yeast
1 1 lb. loaf sour dough bread
2 c. rolled oats
4 ½ c. chicken or turkey broth
2 14 oz. cans whole berry cranberry sauce

1 20 oz. can crushed pineapple
1 29 oz. can canned pumpkin
1 ½ c. whole walnuts
1 ½ c. pecan halves
1 10 oz. pkg. miniature marshmallows
2 6 oz. pkg. raspberry Jell-O™

Staples:

flour	sugar	vegetable oil
baking powder	powdered sugar	olive oil
baking soda	brown sugar	light corn syrup
ground cinnamon	milk	honey
ground nutmeg	eggs	kosher salt
pure vanilla extract	shortening	coarse black pepper

shopping lists available for print online.

CHAPTER FOUR

Home for the Holiday

Etched in my mind are the colors of Christmas
and the feeling of winter warmth. Familiar aromas
from preparing keepsake recipes on Christmas
Eve bring joy as memories come to life. I have
the happiest holiday memories of Christmas Eve
warmed by the fire's quiet glow and reverent
reflections of that Silent Night.

The anticipation of time remembered, flavors
from Christmas past, enhance and entice us to
move forward creating these same expressions of
magical cheer. We gather with family and friends
and so it begins… Christmas is almost here.

Pickled Eggs ⚜

8 eggs

10 mini kosher pickles

1 tsp. yellow mustard

1 tsp. coarse black pepper

4 tbsp. mayonnaise

¼ tsp. Worcestershire sauce

Boil eggs for 6 to 8 minutes. Rinse and let sit in cold water for 10 minutes or until completely cooled. Set aside 2 whole hard-cooked eggs. Peel the remaining eggs and slice in half lengthwise. Remove yolks carefully and place in a small mixing bowl. Place egg halves on a tray. Chop mini pickles into small pieces and add pickles and the 2 whole eggs to the yolks; mash with a fork. Fold in all other ingredients. Fill egg halves with yolk mixture.

Christmas Chop Salad ⚜

1 c. sliced almonds
6 celery stalks
4 baby cucumbers
1 lg. Napa cabbage
2 red apples
2 c. purple grapes
4 green onions
1 c. dried cranberries

Preheat oven to 375°. Spread almonds on a jelly roll pan and bake for 10 to 12 minutes until golden brown.

Clean and chop celery, cucumbers and cabbage; place in a large bowl. Rinse, core and chop apples into small chunks. Rinse and cut grapes in half. Peel and dice green onions. Toss all ingredients together and refrigerate to keep crisp.

Red Wine Vinaigrette ⚜

⅓ c. red wine vinegar	⅓ c. vegetable oil	1 tsp. kosher salt
1 lime, juice	⅓ c. sugar	½ tsp. coarse black pepper

Combine all ingredients in a blender, chill. Toss with Christmas Chop Salad when ready to serve.

Cranberry Pecan Cheese Balls ⚜

2 tsp. butter
3 tbsp. brown sugar
½ c. pecans, chopped

6 oz. cream cheese
⅓ c. dried cranberries, chopped

Preheat oven to 350°. In a small frying pan, melt butter and add brown sugar to form a soft glaze. Fold in pecans and continue to mix until all the nuts are coated. Spread on a small jelly roll pan and bake for 10 to 12 minutes. Remove and chill before breaking up candied pecans.

In a mixing bowl, fold together cream cheese and candied pecans. Finely chop dried cranberries. Form 1-inch balls from cream cheese mixture and roll in chopped cranberries. Cover and chill before serving.

Dill Cheese Balls ⚜

6 oz. cream cheese 4 tsp. fresh dill, minced

1 ½ tsp. onion salt 2 celery stalks

In a mixing bowl, place cream cheese, onion salt and 1 teaspoon fresh dill. Clean and finely dice celery; fold into cream cheese. Form 1-inch balls and roll each cheese ball in remaining dill. Place in covered container and chill. Serve with Baked Pita Chips.

Cheddar Cheese Balls ⚜

6 oz. cream cheese 6 crisp bacon strips

1 ½ tsp. garlic pepper 1 c. sharp cheddar cheese, shredded

In a small mixing bowl, combine cream cheese, garlic pepper, chopped bacon and ⅓ c. sharp cheddar cheese. Form 1-inch cheese balls and roll in remaining cheddar cheese. Cover and chill until ready to serve.

Baked Pita Chips ⚜

4 whole pita pockets olive oil kosher salt

Preheat oven to 400°. Open each pita pocket and spread out flat. Generously brush the inner side of each pocket with olive oil and season with salt. Cut into 1-inch wide strips. Place strips on jelly roll pan and bake for 8 to 10 minutes or until golden brown (as pictured). Do not overbake.

Split Pea Soup ⚜

1 med. white onion	1 tsp. kosher salt	2 c. dry split peas, rinsed
3 celery stalks	1 tsp. coarse black pepper	10 c. chicken broth
3 carrots	2 bay leaves	1 c. heavy whipping cream
2 tbsp. butter	1 tbsp. fresh thyme, minced	12 bacon strips

Peel and dice onion. Rinse and chop celery stalks. Peel and slice carrots. In a large heavy 4-quart pot, melt the butter over medium heat and add salt and pepper. Fold in vegetables and cook until the onion is soft. Add the bay leaves and thyme. Stir in split peas and coat with spices and butter sauce. Gradually add chicken broth and cream. Cover pot and turn down heat; simmer soup over low heat for an hour. Cook bacon until crisp; cut into small pieces. Set aside 2 tablespoons of chopped bacon for garnish and fold remaining bacon into soup.

Parmesan Cheese Rolls ⚜

½ c. butter
1 ½ c. grated Parmesan cheese
2 tsp. kosher salt
1 tsp. parsley flakes
24 frozen rolls

In a medium-size pot, melt butter over medium-low heat. In a mixing bowl, combine cheese, salt and parsley; mix well. Continue to heat butter while placing 4 to 5 frozen rolls in pot at a time. Let rolls rest in hot butter turning 2 to 3 times. Place warm buttered rolls in cheese mixture, turning rolls to completely coat all sides. Use 2 jelly roll pans. Place 12 rolls 2-inches apart on each pan. Let rise according to frozen roll instructions. Preheat oven to 375°. Bake for 12 to 15 minutes or until golden brown.

Lemon Pepper Vegetables ⚜

8 lg. carrots
3 c. fresh thin green beans
4 tbsp. butter
2 tsp. lemon pepper

Peel carrots and cut into large diagonal pieces (as pictured). Snip ends of green beans and rinse. Bring water to a boil in a large stockpot. Place carrots in first and cook 2 minutes. Add green beans and cook for 3 more minutes or until desired tenderness. Rinse in colander and return to pot. Toss with butter and lemon pepper. Place in serving bowl.

Rosemary Chicken ⚜

2 lbs. frozen chicken tenders
¾ c. butter
½ c. flour
4 tbsp. granulated chicken bouillon

2 ½ c. heavy whipping cream
1 ½ c. milk
8 oz. jar marinated artichokes

1 tsp. coarse black pepper
2 tsp. fresh rosemary or 1 tsp. dried
¼ c. white cooking wine

Spray medium-size stockpot with cooking spray. Place frozen chicken tenders in pot on medium-high heat and cover with lid. Let cook, stirring occasionally until the chicken is completely cooked, about 10 to 12 minutes. Remove from heat and set aside. When slightly cooled, pull chicken apart into bite-size pieces.

Melt butter in a heavy stockpot and whisk in flour and chicken bouillon. Stir until crumbly; cook 2 to 3 minutes or until golden brown. Fold in cream and continue to cook. Slowly add milk and marinade from the artichokes. Fold in pepper, rosemary and cooking wine.

Preheat oven to 375°. Place chicken pieces and artichokes in a 9 x 13 baking dish. Pour rosemary sauce over chicken and artichokes. Cover with aluminum foil. Bake for 40 to 50 minutes. Serve over sticky rice.

Sticky Rice ⚜

2 ½ c. water
2 c. sticky rice

Use Calrose rice. In a saucepan, bring water to a boil. Stir in rice and turn heat down to medium-low and cover. Cook without stirring, about 12 to 15 minutes or until liquid is absorbed. Serve with Rosemary Chicken.

Bavarian Apple Torte ⚜

Crust:
- ½ c. butter, softened
- ½ c. sugar
- ¼ tsp. pure vanilla extract
- 1 c. flour

Vanilla Cream filling:
- 16 oz. cream cheese
- ⅓ c. sugar
- 1 egg
- 1 tsp. pure vanilla extract

Topping:
- 4 c. peeled red apples, thinly sliced
- ⅓ c. sugar
- ½ tsp. ground cinnamon

Preheat oven to 450°. Cream butter, sugar and vanilla together and add flour. Press crust into a 9-inch tart pan, pressing crust evenly up on the sides.

In a mixing bowl blend together softened cream cheese, sugar, egg and vanilla. Pour mixture over pastry crust.

Toss thinly sliced apples in sugar and cinnamon. Arrange apple slices on top of cream cheese filling. Bake at 450° for 10 minutes, then reduce heat to 400° and bake for 25 more minutes. Remove from oven, let cool. Refrigerate. When ready to serve place on serving dish and garnish with mint leaves and raspberries.

Garnish:

fresh mint leaves, rinsed   fresh raspberries, rinsed

Details...

Christmas colored chargers set the tone for this elegant meal. Pleasing red and white Christmas dishes dress this evening well.

Details...

A table set with tradition starts with a natural Noel wreath made by simply winding a cedar garland into a small circle. Tied with a bow, attached to the back of each chair, is just the right scent of pine to enhance this fireside feast.

Details...

Simple pomegranates parade across this tablescape with regal candles to create a warm welcome. The hint of pine mingled with relaxing conversation captures the moment for treasured memories that become keepsakes held dear.

Shopping List

Each recipe is designed to serve eight to ten

18 crisp bacon strips
2 lbs. frozen chicken tenders
3 ½ c. heavy whipping cream
34 oz. cream cheese
1 lb. butter
1 c. sharp cheddar cheese
1 ½ c. grated Parmesan cheese
11 lg. carrots
3 c. fresh thin green beans
1 med. white onion
11 celery stalks
4 baby cucumbers
1 lg. head Napa cabbage
6 red apples

2 c. purple grapes
4 green onions
1 ⅓ c. dried cranberries
1 lime
1 sm. bunch fresh mint leaves
1 sm. container fresh
raspberries
1 tbsp. fresh thyme
2 tsp. fresh rosemary
or 1 tsp. dried
4 tsp. fresh dill
2 bay leaves
2 tsp. lemon pepper
1 ½ tsp. garlic pepper

1 tsp. parsley flakes
2 c. Calrose rice
4 whole pita pockets
24 frozen rolls
⅓ c. red wine vinegar
¼ c. white cooking wine
10 c. chicken broth
4 tbsp. granulated chicken bouillon
2 c. dry split peas
10 mini kosher pickles
1 8 oz. jar marinated artichokes
1 c. sliced almonds
½ c. chopped pecans

Staples:

flour
ground cinnamon
pure vanilla extract
sugar
brown sugar

milk
eggs
vegetable oil
olive oil
kosher salt

onion salt
coarse black pepper
Worcestershire sauce
yellow mustard
mayonnaise

shopping lists available for print online.

CHAPTER FIVE

Merry & Bright

Make your Christmas morning Merry and Bright with this selection of brunch recipes. Most of this Christmas brunch can be prepared ahead of time and warmed to perfection just before serving. Quiche is always better the second day as the flavors are allowed to deepen. Trifle desserts can be made the day before and simply chilled. Let Oven Roasted French Onion Soup simmer in the oven while gifts are exchanged.

Some moments are part of our lives forever. This cozy brunch will have a timeless appeal as children return home and welcomed guests arrive. We hope this Merry and Bright Christmas Brunch will reawaken traditions from the kitchen and become a timeless treasure.

Salami & Cheddar Pretzel Bites ⚜

2 tbsp. brown sugar	1–2 tbsp. olive oil	6 c. water
1 c. milk, warm	1 c. sliced salami, finely chopped	4 tsp baking soda
2 ½ c. flour	1 c. shredded cheddar cheese	1–2 tbsp. sea salt
1 pkg. instant dry yeast		

In a mixing bowl combine, brown sugar and warm milk. Stir until sugar is dissolved. Add flour and yeast to milk mixture and stir until dough forms. Add more flour as needed. Turn out dough on a lightly floured surface and gently knead, forming a smooth ball.

Brush the sides of another bowl with olive oil and transfer dough. Cover the bowl tightly with plastic wrap and allow to rise in a warm place for 2 hours or until dough has doubled in size and is light and bubbly.

Place the dough onto a lightly floured surface. Divide into 4 equal parts. Roll out each piece of dough into 12 x 4-inch strips. Combine salami and cheddar cheese and place along the edge of the dough strip, lengthwise. Roll each strip tightly and Cut into 1-inch thick pretzel bites.

In a large pot over high heat, bring water to a boil and add baking soda. Reduce heat to a simmer. Place 5 to 6 pretzel bites at a time in the boiling water. Boil for 20 to 25 seconds, turning one time. Remove from water and place on parchment-lined jelly roll pans for baking. Repeat until all pretzel bites are boiled.

Preheat oven to 400°. Sprinkle pretzel bites with sea salt and bake for 12 to 15 minutes or until puffy and golden brown. Serve with warm Cheddar Dipping Sauce.

Cheddar Dipping Sauce ⚜

2 tbsp. butter
2 tbsp. flour
1 tsp. salt
1 c. milk
1 c. sharp cheddar cheese, shredded
1 tsp. yellow mustard
1 tsp. garlic pepper
salt and pepper to taste

In a saucepan, melt butter on medium-high. Whisk in flour and salt stirring continually. Slowly fold in milk. Whisk in cheese, mustard and garlic pepper until cheese is melted and sauce is smooth. Add salt and pepper to taste. Serve warm.

Onion Cheddar Bread ⚜

1 ½ c. flour
3 tsp. baking powder
1 tsp. kosher salt
2 tbsp. butter, softened
1 c. shredded sharp cheddar cheese, divided
1 tbsp. olive oil
4 green onion
1 egg
½ c. milk

Preheat oven to 400°. Prepare an 8-inch round baking dish with cooking spray. Combine flour, baking powder and salt in a medium-size mixing bowl. Cut butter into flour until mixture is crumbly; add ½ c. sharp cheddar cheese.

Heat olive oil in skillet over medium high heat. Dice the green onion and lightly fry in olive oil, 1 to 2 minutes and set aside.

In a small mixing bowl, beat egg and milk together. Add cooked onion and pour into flour mixture. Stir until just moist. The dough will be soft and sticky.

Place dough in prepared baking dish and top with remaining ½ c. sharp cheddar cheese. Bake for 20 to 25 minutes or until golden on top. Slice and serve warm with Sour Cream Butter.

Sour Cream Butter ⚜

¼ c. butter, softened
¼ c. sour cream
1 tsp. onion salt
¼ tsp. parsley flakes

Whip all ingredients together until light and fluffy. Chill. Serve with Onion Cheddar Bread.

Veggie Quiche ⚜

Crust:

1 ½ c. sifted flour
½ tsp. kosher salt

½ c. + 1 tbsp. shortening

7 tbsp. ice water

or 1 frozen pastry sheet or pie crust

Preheat oven to 425°. In a medium-size bowl, whisk flour and salt together. Cut in shortening, using a pastry blender, until crumbly pea-size pieces form. Sprinkle with cold water. Using a fork, toss until dough is moist and forms a soft ball.

Place the dough on a lightly floured surface. With a floured rolling pin, roll out a ¼-inch thick circle. Fold dough in half and place in a quiche pan. Unfold and press firmly against bottom and sides. Trim overhanging edges of dough.

Bake 8 to 10 minutes. Remove pie crust from oven and reduce temperature to 325°.

Filling:

1 white onion
4 oz. pkg. button mushrooms
1 red bell pepper
1 bundle asparagus

2 tbsp. butter
2 c. shredded Swiss cheese
4 lg. eggs

1 c. heavy whipping cream
1 tsp. kosher salt
¼ tsp. coarse black pepper

Peel and chop onion. Clean and slice mushrooms. Clean, seed and dice bell pepper. Cut off the bottom 2 inches of asparagus and discard. Rinse and chop spears into small pieces. Melt butter over medium high heat in a large skillet. Sauté onions and mushrooms for 2 minutes. Add other veggies and continue to sauté for 1 to 2 minutes. Sprinkle sautéed veggies and Swiss cheese in the bottom of the baked crust.

In a medium-size bowl, beat eggs and stir in cream, salt and pepper. Pour egg mixture over veggies and cheese. Bake for 45 to 50 minutes or until knife inserted in center comes out clean. Extra cooking time may vary depending on moisture from vegetables. Let stand 10 minutes before serving.

Classic Quiche Lorraine ⚜

Crust:

1 ½ c. flour

½ tsp. kosher salt

½ c. + 1 tbsp. shortening

7 tbsp. ice water

or 1 frozen pastry sheet or pie crust

Preheat oven to 425°. In a medium-size bowl, whisk flour and salt together. Cut in shortening, using a pastry blender, until crumbly pea-size pieces form. Sprinkle with cold water. Using a fork, toss until dough is moist and forms a soft ball.

Place the dough on a lightly floured surface. With a floured rolling pin, roll out a ¼-inch thick circle. Fold dough in half and place in a quiche pan. Unfold and press firmly against bottom and sides. Trim overhanging edges of dough.

Bake 8 to 10 minutes. Remove pie crust from oven and reduce temperature to 325°.

Filling:

12 slices crisp cooked bacon
4 green onions, divided
1 c. shredded Swiss cheese

4 lg. eggs
2 c. heavy whipping cream
½ tsp. kosher salt

¼ tsp. coarse black pepper
⅛ tsp. cayenne pepper

Crumble cooked bacon and thinly slice green onions. Set aside 1 tbsp. of green onions for garnish. Sprinkle bacon, cheese and green onions on the bottom of the baked crust. Beat eggs in a medium-size bowl and add cream and seasonings; stir and pour over bacon, cheese and onions. Bake 45 to 50 minutes or until knife inserted in center comes out clean. Let stand 10 minutes before serving. Garnish with sliced green onions.

Italian Basil Quiche ⚜

Crust:

1 ½ c. flour   ½ c. + 1 tbsp. shortening   7 tbsp. ice water
½ tsp. kosher salt

or 1 frozen pastry sheet or pie crust

Preheat oven to 425°. In a medium-size bowl, whisk flour and salt together. Cut in shortening, using a pastry blender, until crumbly pea-size pieces form. Sprinkle with cold water. Using a fork, toss until dough is moist and forms a soft ball.

Place the dough on a lightly floured surface. With a floured rolling pin, roll out a ¼-inch thick circle. Fold dough in half and place in a quiche pan. Unfold and press firmly against bottom and sides. Trim overhanging edges of dough.

Bake 8 to 10 minutes. Remove pie crust from oven and reduce temperature to 325°.

Filling:

- 12 oz. spicy ground Italian sausage
- 1 ½ c. shredded mozzarella cheese
- 4 green onion, finely chopped
- 3 sm. yellow peppers, diced
- 3 sm. red peppers, diced
- ½ c. fresh basil, chopped
- 4 lg. eggs
- 2 c. heavy whipping cream
- ½ tsp. garlic pepper
- ½ tsp. kosher salt
- ¼ tsp. coarse black pepper

Brown sausage in a frying pan over medium high heat for 8 to 10 minutes. Place cooked sausage in bottom of baked pie crust and add cheese, onions, peppers and basil. In a medium-size bowl, whisk eggs, cream, garlic pepper, salt and pepper together. Pour over veggies in pie crust. Bake for 45 to 50 minutes or until knife inserted in center comes out clean. Let stand 10 minutes before serving.

Potato Crusted Jalapeño Quiche ⚜

Crust:

2 tsp. olive oil	¼ tsp. coarse black pepper	1 c. shredded Mexican blend cheese
¼ tsp. kosher salt	3 c. frozen shredded hash browns	

Preheat oven to 425°. In a frying pan, heat olive oil, salt and pepper. When olive oil is hot, add frozen hash browns. Spread out evenly and coat potatoes with hot olive oil. Cover the pan. After cooking for 3 to 4 minutes, turn over hash browns and cook an additional 3 to 4 minutes; repeat until hash browns are fully cooked. Fold in 1 c. shredded cheese and let cool. Line a quiche pan with cooked hash browns; press into bottom, up sides and on edges of pan. Spread 3 c. shredded cheese on the bottom of the potato crust.

Filling:

3 c. shredded Mexican blend cheese
½ jalapeño, with seeds
3 Roma tomatoes, divided

½ c. cilantro, minced
3 eggs
1 c. evaporated milk

½ tsp. kosher salt
½ tsp. coarse black pepper

Rinse and chop jalapeno, and 2 tomatoes. Rinse and mince cilantro. Whisk eggs, evaporated milk, salt and pepper. Add jalapeno, tomatoes and cilantro to egg mixture and pour over cheese in the crust. Bake for 40 to 50 minutes or until a knife is clean when inserted in center. Slice remaining tomato for garnish and serve.

Shrimp Zucchini Quiche ⚜

Crust:

1 ½ c. flour   ½ c. + 1 tbsp. shortening   7 tbsp. ice water
½ tsp. kosher salt

or 1 frozen pastry sheet or pie crust

Preheat oven to 425°. In a medium-size bowl, whisk flour and salt together. Cut in shortening, using a pastry blender, until crumbly pea-size pieces form. Sprinkle with cold water. Using a fork, toss until dough is moist and forms a soft ball.

Place the dough on a lightly floured surface. With a floured rolling pin, roll out a ¼-inch thick circle. Fold dough in half and place in a quiche pan. Unfold and press firmly against bottom and sides. Trim overhanging edges of dough.

Bake 8 to 10 minutes. Remove pie crust from oven and reduce temperature to 325°.

Filling:

2 c. cooked bay shrimp	1 ½ c. shredded Monterey Jack cheese	½ tsp. kosher salt
1 sm. yellow onion	4 lg. eggs	¼ tsp. coarse black pepper
2 sm. zucchini	2 c. heavy whipping cream	⅓ c. sour cream, garnish

Rinse shrimp and set aside. Peel and chop onion. Core and dice zucchini. Place shrimp, onions, zucchini and cheese on the bottom of the baked pie crust. In a medium-size bowl, beat eggs. Fold in cream, salt and pepper; pour over shrimp, cheese and veggies. Bake 45 to 50 minutes or until knife inserted in center comes out clean. Let stand 10 minutes before serving and garnish with sour cream.

Oven Roasted French Onion Soup ⚜

4 tbsp. butter
3 lg. yellow onions
4 cloves garlic
1 ½ tsp. kosher salt
2 c. beef broth
¾ c. red wine vinegar
1 ½ tbsp. Worcestershire sauce
1 ½ tbsp. balsamic vinegar
1 tsp. paprika
1 tsp. dried thyme
½ tsp. coarse black pepper
½ loaf French baguette
1-2 tbsp. olive oil
½-1 lb. sliced Swiss cheese

Heat butter in a large pot over medium heat. Peel and thinly slice onions and mince garlic. Add onions and garlic to butter; sprinkle with salt and sauté for 15 to 20 minutes or until caramelized. Stir in beef broth, vinegar, Worcestershire sauce, balsamic vinegar, paprika, thyme and pepper.

Preheat oven to broil. Slice baguette into ¼-inch thick slices and brush with olive oil. Place slices on a jelly roll pan and broil each side until golden brown.

Lower the oven temperature to 375°. Pour the onion soup into a 9 x 13 baking dish. Arrange bread slices over soup (as pictured) and top with Swiss cheese. Place in oven for 10 to 15 minutes until cheese is golden brown and crisp on the edges. Serve from baking dish with a ladle into small serving bowls.

Orange Ginger Trifle ⚜

½ c. butter-flavored shortening
⅓ c. sugar
1 c. molasses
¾ c. water

1 egg
2⅓ c. flour
1 tsp. baking soda

1 tsp. ground ginger
1 tsp. ground cinnamon
¾ tsp. kosher salt

Preheat oven to 350°. In a large bowl, cream shortening and sugar until light and fluffy. Continue beating while adding the molasses, water and egg. In another bowl, whisk together the flour, baking soda, ginger, cinnamon and salt; add to cream mixture and beat until combined.

Pour into a greased jelly roll pan. Bake for 18 to 22 minutes or until a toothpick inserted in the center comes out clean. Cool on a wire rack. Cut the entire pan of gingerbread into small bite-size squares and set aside.

Orange Sauce:
    1 c. sugar
    1¼ c. heavy whipping cream

¼ c. orange juice

2 drops orange food coloring

In a small saucepan, combine the sugar, cream, orange juice and orange food coloring; whisk together over medium-high heat. Bring ingredients to a boil and turn down heat. Let simmer for 3 to 5 minutes, stirring occasionally. Remove from heat and chill before assembling trifle.

Toppings:
    2 16 oz. frozen whipped topping
    2 4 oz. Ghirardelli™ white chocolate baking bar, chopped

1 orange, zest

Cover bottom of trifle bowl with gingerbread squares and drizzle with Orange Sauce. Sprinkle a layer of white chocolate chunks and add dollops of whipped topping. Repeat additional layers, finishing with whipped topping. Garnish with orange zest and a sprinkle of chopped white chocolate. Refrigerate until ready to serve.

Lemon Poppy Seed Pound Cake ⚜

1 butter cake mix
1 3.9 oz. pkg. instant vanilla pudding
4 eggs

¾ c. vegetable oil
¾ c. water, warm

¼ c. heavy whipping cream
¼ c. poppy seeds

Preheat oven to 350°. In a mixing bowl, combine all ingredients together and mix well. Prepare a bundt pan, or wreath bundt pan (as pictured), with cooking spray. Pour batter into prepared baking pan and bake for 50 to 60 minutes or when toothpick inserted in center comes out clean. Cool cake slightly before turning out on a serving plate.

Lemon Glaze ⚜

3 tbsp. lemon juice
6 tbsp. powdered sugar
1½ c. fresh raspberries, garnish

Whisk together lemon juice and sugar. While still warm; drizzle Lemon Glaze over pound cake. Chill. Garnish with fresh raspberries before serving.

Chocolate Brownie Trifle ⚜

1 brownie mix
1 ½ c. white chocolate chips
2 5.9 oz. pkg. instant chocolate pudding
5 c. milk
3 c. fresh strawberries
2 16 oz. frozen whipped topping, divided

Prepare your favorite brownie mix. Sprinkle white chocolate chips on top of batter and bake according to directions. Chill before cutting into small bite-size squares.

Prepare chocolate pudding, following the directions for the pie filling. When pudding is set, fold in ½ of 1 of the frozen whipped toppings and mix until smooth. Clean and slice strawberries.

Begin layering trifle with pudding. Add layers of brownie squares, strawberries and whipped topping. Repeat layers. Finish with whipped topping and garnish with strawberries.

Vanilla Pomegranate Trifle ⚜

1 tbsp. water
1 ½ c. walnuts, chopped
⅓ c. sugar, divided
2 5.9 oz. pkg. instant vanilla pudding

5 c. milk
2 16 oz. frozen whipped topping, divided
2 c. pomegranate seeds
1 ready-made angel food cake

In a frying pan, on medium-high, place water, ¼ cup sugar and chopped walnuts, stirring to coat evenly. Stir constantly for 3 to 4 minutes. Place walnuts on a jelly roll pan and sprinkle with remaining sugar to crystallize before cooling. Set aside.

Mix instant pudding according to the directions for pie filling. When pudding is set, fold in ½ of 1 of the whipped toppings and mix until smooth. Cut angel food cake into bite-size pieces.

Assemble the trifle by layering the cake, pudding, whipped topping, pomegranate seeds and sugared walnuts. Repeat layering. Finish with whipped topping and nuts. Chill before serving.

Details...

Vintage Santas and whimsical reindeer surround this Christmas brunch. Familiar names of favorite reindeer line each serving dish.

CHAPTER SIX

Deck the Halls

Every year as Christmas approaches, I feel
a deep sense of gratitude and grace. For me,
celebrating the birth and life of the Savior of the
world makes it such a sacred time. We pause to
give thanks for His humble birth, perfect example
and infinite love. It is the time I feel most hopeful
for change, for peace on earth, good will to men.
It is a season to give and to share. Indeed, it is my
favorite time of the year, and I long for
these feelings to linger.

Whether you celebrate this season with
traditional ceremony or simply find it a time to
gather with family and friends to exchange warm
wishes, I hope these timeless flavors of holidays
past will help you to spread good will.

Artichoke Cheese Crostini ⚜

1 loaf garlic artisan bread
1 6 oz. jar marinated artichoke hearts
1 c. grated Parmesan cheese

½ c. butter, softened
1 tsp. parsley flakes
½ tsp. kosher salt

Preheat oven to broil. Slice artisan bread loaf crosswise. Place slices on a jelly roll pan and toast on both sides. Drain artichoke marinade and chop hearts into small pieces. Combine artichoke hearts, Parmesan cheese, butter, parsley flakes and salt; spread over toasted bread slices.

Return to oven and broil an additional 2 to 3 minutes or until cheese melts and edges are golden and crisp. Serve.

Apple Pomegranate Salad ⚜

2 c. walnuts, chopped
½ c. sugar
1 tbsp. water
10 celery stalks
2 red apples
20 oz. bag spring mix
2 c. pomegranate seeds
12 oz. feta cheese or blue cheese

Place chopped walnuts in a frying pan over medium-high heat. Sprinkle with sugar and stir. Drizzle water over walnuts and continue to cook until sugar coated.

Clean and dice celery. Rinse, core and cut apples into small pieces. In a serving bowl, place spring mix and toss with sugared walnuts, celery, apples, pomegranate seeds and crumbled cheese. Chill before serving.

Sweet Pomegranate Dressing ⚜

1 c. mayonnaise
½ c. sugar
½ c. pomegranate vinegar
½ tsp. onion salt

Combine all ingredients in a blender and mix well. Chill before serving. Serve with Apple Pomegranate Salad.

Oven Roasted Yams ⚜

4 lg. yams	¾ tsp. curry powder	1 ½ tsp. coarse black pepper
3 egg whites	¾ tsp. chili powder	1 4 oz. jar capers
3 tbsp. olive oil	2 tsp. kosher salt	

Preheat oven to 425°. Peel yams and slice into cubes, (as pictured) and place in medium mixing bowl. Separate the whites and yolks from 3 eggs. Put egg whites, olive oil, curry powder, chili powder, salt and pepper in a small bowl and whisk together. Pour egg mixture over yams and toss.

Spread coated yams on a jelly roll pan and bake for 20 minutes. Turn yams and bake an additional 10 to 15 minutes or until tender. Place in a serving bowl and toss with capers. Serve.

Brussels Sprouts Medley ⚜

6 oz. pkg. wild rice	2 tsp. onion salt	12 oz. crumbled blue cheese
2 lbs. Brussels sprouts	½ c. white wine vinegar	½ tsp. coarse black pepper
2 tbsp. olive oil	2 c. pecans halves, chopped	¼ tsp. kosher salt

Cook wild rice according to directions on package. Clean and cut Brussels sprouts in half. Heat olive oil in a large skillet over medium-high heat. Place Brussels sprouts flat side down and scorch. Sprinkle with onion salt. Pour white wine vinegar over the Brussels sprouts. Cover skillet and lower heat; steam for 3 to 5 minutes. Toss rice, Brussels sprouts, pecans and blue cheese together. Place in a serving dish and season with salt and pepper. Serve.

Beef Wellington ⚜

2 puff pastry sheets, frozen
4 tbsp. olive oil, divided
2 beef tenderloins, 2 ½–3 lbs. each
2 tsp. kosher salt, divided
1 tsp. dried rosemary
4 tbsp. butter, divided
1 bundle asparagus
4 c. fresh button mushrooms, divided
8 lg. slices of prosciutto
4 tbsp. Grey Poupon™ mustard
2 egg whites
1 c. cherry tomatoes
1 tsp. coarse black pepper
1 16 oz. pkg. baby spinach
3 1 oz. pkgs. brown gravy mix

Thaw frozen pastry sheets in refrigerator. Rub beef tenderloins with 2 tablespoons olive oil and season with 1 teaspoon salt and rosemary. Drizzle 2 tablespoons of olive oil in a heavy stockpot, over medium-high heat. Sear tenderloins on all sides. Set aside. Add 2 tablespoons of butter to pot and melt. Rinse and remove bottom 2 inches of asparagus and chop into small pieces. Clean and dice 2 cups of mushrooms. Sauté asparagus and mushrooms in butter for 3 to 5 minutes. Set aside.

Place 2 large pieces of plastic wrap on a work surface. On each piece of plastic place prosciutto making rectangles larger than the tenderloins. Spread Grey Poupon™ mustard evenly over the pieces of prosciutto. Spread sautéed asparagus and mushrooms evenly on Prosciutto. Place the seared tenderloins in the center of prosciutto. Using the plastic wrap to cover the tenderloin with prosciutto, wrap plastic tightly around each beef tenderloin and place in the refrigerator for 30 minutes.

Preheat oven to 425°. Roll out 2 sheets of puff pastry about ¼-inch thick. Remove chilled tenderloins from refrigerator and take off plastic wrap. Place tenderloins in the center of each pastry sheet.

Separate the whites and yolks from 2 eggs and whisk egg whites in a small bowl.

Wrap pastry around tenderloins. Brush edges of pastry with egg whites and fold edges under to seal. Place tenderloins 4-inches apart on a greased baking sheet.

Bush tops of pastry with egg whites and sprinkle with 1 teaspoon of salt. Cut diagonal slits (as pictured) on the top of each Beef Wellington to help release steam as it cooks. Bake 25 to 30 minutes. Remove from oven and let rest for 10 minutes before slicing. Serve warm.

In a frying pan melt 2 tablespoons butter. Rinse and cut cherry tomatoes in half and slice remaining cleaned mushrooms. Sauté in melted butter and season with salt and pepper to taste. Place both tenderloins on a spinach-lined serving tray and garnish with sautéed tomatoes and mushrooms.

Because there are no drippings from tenderloins, prepare gravy according to directions on package.

Christmas Cranberry Cake ⚜

2 c. flour
2 c. sugar
2 tsp. baking soda
1 29 oz. can pears
2 eggs, beaten
1 10 oz. bag fresh cranberries, rinsed

Preheat oven to 350°. In a mixing bowl, whisk together flour, sugar and baking soda. Mash pears with juice into small chunks using a potato masher. Fold into flour mixture and add beaten eggs. Stir in cranberries and mix well. Prepare a 9 x 13 baking dish with cooking spray and pour batter into dish. Bake for 45 to 50 minutes or until toothpick inserted in the center comes out clean.

Whipped Cream:
  1 ½ c. heavy whipping cream
  ⅓ c. sugar
  2 tsp. pure vanilla extract

Place whipping cream in a chilled bowl and whip with an electric mixer on high until stiff peaks form. Fold in sugar and vanilla; whip for an additional 30 seconds. Chill until ready to serve.

Vanilla Caramel Sauce ⚜

¾ c. butter

1 c. sugar

¾ c. heavy whipping cream

1 ½ tsp. pure vanilla extract

Melt butter in a small saucepan over medium heat. Add sugar and cream. Bring to a boil. Turn down heat and simmer for 10 to 12 minutes. Remove from heat and add vanilla. Serve with Christmas Cranberry Cake and fresh Whipped Cream.

Details...

Here is where tradition, elegance and memories meet. A joyous spirit and seasonal splendor dress the table. This merry, merry mix of flavors will bring magic to your holiday gathering.

Details...

Many shades of Christmas... The chandelier is adorned with bright colored ornaments that are festive yet classic and cast a holiday cheer with dazzling brilliance.

Notes & Comments

Shopping List

Each recipe is designed to serve twelve plus

2 beef tenderloins, 2 ½–3 lbs. ea.

8 lg. slices prosciutto

12 oz. crumbled blue cheese

12 oz. feta cheese or blue cheese

1 c. grated Parmesan cheese

2 ¼ c. heavy whipping cream

2 puff pastry sheets, frozen

1 bundle asparagus

4 c. fresh button mushrooms

1 c. cherry tomatoes

1 16 oz. pkg. baby spinach

2 lbs. Brussels sprouts

10 celery stalks

2 red apples

20 oz. bag spring mix

2 c. pomegranate seeds

4 lg. yams

1 10 oz. bag fresh cranberries

1 tsp. dried rosemary

¾ tsp. curry powder

¾ tsp. chili powder

1 tsp. parsley flakes

1 6 oz. box wild rice

1 loaf garlic artisan bread

4 tbsp. Grey Poupon™ mustard

3 pkgs. 1 oz. brown gravy mix

½ c. white wine vinegar

½ c. pomegranate vinegar

1 29 oz. can pears

2 c. pecans halves

2 c. walnuts

1 4 oz. jar capers

1 6 oz. jar marinated artichoke hearts

Staples:

flour	butter	onion salt
baking soda	eggs	coarse black pepper
pure vanilla extract	olive oil	mayonnaise
sugar	kosher salt	

shopping lists available for print online.

Gifts from the Kitchen

Love, The Huxtables

CHAPTER SEVEN

Gifts from the Kitchen

The art of giving is truly something my good friends have mastered. Many of these sweet treats have shown up at my door as a token of friendship. Gifts of good taste include forgotten family favorites that can be shared again and again. All are simple expressions of affection.

This chapter, filled with homemade-with-heart care packages has something for everyone on your list. Delivering fresh-from-the-oven goodness spreads holiday cheer. Enhance the pleasure of giving and wrap up the season with Gifts From the Kitchen.

Almond Bark ⚜

1 c. butter
½ c. sugar
2 pkgs. Graham crackers
1 c. sliced almonds
1 tsp. kosher salt

Preheat oven to 375°. In a medium-size pot melt butter. Add sugar and boil for 2 minutes.

Line a jelly roll pan with graham crackers and pour butter and sugar mixture over crackers. Spread sliced almonds evenly over the crackers and sprinkle with salt.

Bake for 10 minutes. Cool and break or cut into triangles (as pictured) and serve.

With Love,
The Huxtables

Easy Fudge ⚜

3 c. semisweet or milk chocolate chips
1 14 oz. can sweetened condensed milk
¼ c. butter
1 tsp. pure vanilla extract

Prepare an 8 x 8 glass dish with cooking spray and set aside. Combine chocolate chips, sweetened condensed milk and butter in a glass bowl. Heat in the microwave for 20 seconds at a time, stirring between, until completely melted. Do not overcook. Fold in vanilla. Pour fudge into prepared dish and place in refrigerator for 2 hours or until set. Cut into squares and serve.

Spiced Maple Syrup ⚜

1 c. water
1 c. sugar
1 c. brown sugar
1 tsp. pure maple extract
¼ tsp. ground cloves
¼ tsp. ground allspice
¼ tsp. ground cinnamon

Bring water to a boil in a medium-size saucepan. Add sugars and stir to dissolve. Reduce heat to low and stir in maple extract, cloves, allspice and cinnamon. Simmer for 2 to 3 minutes and remove from heat. Let cool.

Blueberry Waffle Mix ⚜

3 ⅓ c. flour
⅔ c. nonfat dry milk
6 tsp. sugar
3 tsp. baking powder
3 tsp. baking soda
3 tsp. kosher salt
1 ½ c. dried blueberries

Combine all ingredients in a large bowl and whisk together. Place dried blueberries in bottom of glass jar and top with waffle mix. Place in an airtight container. Give the Blueberry Waffle Mix and a pitcher or jar of homemade syrup as a gift with the following instructions:

Instructions: In a bowl, whisk together 2 ½ cup water, 4 tablespoons vegetable oil and 4 eggs. Add Blueberry Waffle Mix and stir. Heat waffle maker and cook waffles until golden brown. Serve with Spiced Maple Syrup or Cinnamon Buttermilk Syrup.

Pancake Mix ⚜

3 ⅓ c. flour

⅔ c. nonfat dry milk

6 tsp. sugar

3 tsp. baking powder

3 tsp. baking soda

3 tsp. kosher salt

1 tsp. ground cinnamon

½ tsp. ground nutmeg

Combine all ingredients in a large bowl and whisk together. Place pancake mix in an airtight container. Give the Pancake Mix with a pitcher or jar of homemade syrup as a gift with the following instructions:

Instructions: In a bowl, whisk together 2 ½ cups water, 4 tablespoons vegetable oil and 2 eggs. Add Pancake Mix and stir. Heat griddle on medium-high and cook pancakes until golden brown. Serve with Spiced Maple Syrup or Cinnamon Buttermilk Syrup.

Cinnamon Buttermilk Syrup ⚜

1 ½ c. butter

2 ¼ c. sugar

1 tsp. ground cinnamon

1 ½ c. buttermilk

1 tbsp. pure vanilla extract

1 tbsp. baking soda

In a large pot over medium heat, melt butter. Add sugar, cinnamon and buttermilk and stir well. As it begins to boil, turn heat down and let simmer for 3 to 4 minutes. Remove from heat and whisk in vanilla and baking soda. The syrup will foam immediately; keep stirring and let stand. Serve warm or cool and pour into individual jars for gifting.

Helpful Hint: Cinnamon Buttermilk Syrup may be refrigerated up to 4 weeks.

Vanilla Peanut Butter Cookies ⚜

½ c. shortening
½ c. sugar
¼ c. brown sugar
1 egg
1 tbsp. water
2 tsp. pure vanilla extract
1½ c. flour
¼ tsp. ground cinnamon
¼ tsp. kosher salt
½ tsp. baking soda
¾ c. peanut butter chips

In a large mixing bowl, combine shortening, sugars, egg, water and vanilla together. Mix with an electric mixer until creamy. In a separate mixing bowl combine flour, cinnamon, salt and baking soda and add to creamed mixture until just combined. Fold in peanut butter chips and chill dough in the refrigerator for 30 minutes.

Preheat oven to 375° and prepare 2 jelly roll pans with cooking spray or line with parchment paper. Scoop dough into balls, using a large cookie scoop; place on prepared pans 2-inches apart and bake for 8 to 10 minutes. Cool on racks and serve.

Tall Timbers ⚜

½ c. shortening
½ c. sugar
½ c. molasses
½ tsp. white vinegar
1 egg, beaten
3 c. flour
½ tsp. baking soda
¼ tsp. kosher salt
1 tsp. ground cinnamon
1 tsp. ground ginger
½ tsp. ground nutmeg

In a heavy pot, on medium heat bring shortening, sugar, molasses and vinegar to a boil, stirring constantly. Remove from heat to cool down. When mixture is warm, whisk in egg.

Whisk flour before measuring. In a large bowl, whisk all dry ingredients together and add to warm mixture, stirring until a soft dough forms.

Preheat oven to 375°. Prepare jelly roll pans with cooking spray or use parchment paper. On a lightly floured surface, roll out dough ¼-inch thick. Use a large tree cookie cutter to cut dough into tree shapes. Place trees on pans 1-inch apart. Bake for 5 to 6 minutes. Do not overbake. Remove cookies from pans and place on a cooling rack for 3 to 5 minutes. Store in airtight containers to keep cookies soft.

Shortbread Caramel Chews ⚜

³/₄ c. butter, softened
³/₄ c. sugar
2 egg yolks

½ tsp. pure vanilla extract
¼ tsp. kosher salt
2 c. flour

Homemade Caramel (p. 128)
1 c. semisweet chocolate chips

Combine butter, sugar, egg yolks, vanilla and salt in a medium-size mixing bowl and cream together. Fold in flour, handling as little as possible. Chill dough in refrigerator for 30 minutes.

Preheat oven to 325°. Remove dough from refrigerator. Using mini muffin pans with 1-inch wide cups, press teaspoon-size scoops of dough into each cup. Bake 15 to 18 minutes. Remove from oven and drizzle a ½ to ³/₄ teaspoon of hot Homemade Caramel over each shortbread cup and place 4 or 5 chocolate chips on top. Let cool completely before serving.

Snowball Cookies ⚜

1 ½ c. flour
¾ c. unsweetened cocoa powder
2 tsp. baking powder
¾ tsp. kosher salt
½ c. butter, softened
¾ c. brown sugar
¼ c. sugar
2 eggs
1 tsp. pure vanilla extract
1 ¼ c. semisweet chocolate chips
1 c. powdered sugar, for coating

Combine flour, cocoa, baking powder and salt in a medium-size bowl. In a separate bowl cream together butter and sugars with an electric mixer. Add eggs and vanilla and blend well. Add flour mixture to creamed mixture and mix until a soft dough forms. Fold in chocolate chips. Cover dough and place in the refrigerator for 1 hour.

Preheat oven to 350°. Prepare jelly roll pans with cooking spray or line with parchment paper. Place powdered sugar in a small bowl. Using a cookie scoop, make tablespoon-size balls with chilled dough; roll in powdered sugar. Place balls 2 inches apart on prepared pans. Bake cookies for 10 to 12 minutes. Cookies will puff up and crack.

You Joy! Love The Huxtables

Homemade Caramel ⚜

½ c. butter
2 c. brown sugar
1 c. light corn syrup
1 14 oz. can sweetened condensed milk
1 tsp. pure vanilla extract

In a saucepan, melt butter over medium heat. Add sugar and corn syrup, stirring constantly. Bring to a boil and lower heat. Slowly add condensed milk and continue to stir as mixture simmers. When caramel reaches a soft-ball stage, remove from heat and stir in vanilla.

Helpful Hint: To test for a soft-ball stage, drizzle a little hot caramel into a small bowl of cold water and use your fingers to form a soft ball that holds together slightly.

Caramel Popcorn ⚜

Homemade Caramel

16 oz. bag hot air popped buttery popcorn

Place the popcorn in a large mixing bowl. Stir while pouring warm caramel over popcorn. While still warm, place desired amounts of Caramel Popcorn into serving dish or gift packages, but do not seal until caramel has cooled.

White Chocolate Lemon Truffles ⚜

⅓ c. + 1 tbsp. heavy whipping cream
2 tsp. lemon extract
9 oz. white chocolate baking bars
⅛ tsp. kosher salt
4 tbsp. butter
1 c. powdered sugar
1 tbsp. lemon juice
½ c. sugar, for coating

In a small saucepan over medium heat, combine cream and lemon extract. Chop white chocolate baking bars and add to saucepan. Add salt and butter to saucepan, stirring constantly. When mixture begins to simmer, whisk in powdered sugar and lemon juice. Stir mixture over heat until sugar is dissolved, 2 to 3 minutes. Remove from heat and place in a glass bowl to cool. Cover and chill in refrigerator for 4 hours.

Place sugar in a small bowl. Remove truffle base from refrigerator. Using a small cookie scoop or small spoon, form balls. Roll the balls in sugar until well coated to form truffles (as pictured). Store in the refrigerator before serving.

Cranberry Coconut Squares

4 eggs
1 c. butter, softened
2 c. sugar
2 c. flour
2 tsp. coconut extract
1 ½ c. sweetened flake coconut, divided
1 ½ c. white chocolate chips, divided
1 c. dried cranberries

Preheat oven to 350°. Prepare a 9 x 13 baking dish with cooking spray. Beat eggs in a medium-size bowl. Fold in butter, sugar, flour and coconut extract. Gently stir with a fork until just combined.

Fold in ½ cup sweetened flake coconut and ½ cup white chocolate chips. Pour batter into the baking dish and sprinkle with dried cranberries and remaining white chocolate chips and coconut.

Bake for 20 to 25 minutes or until toothpick inserted in the center comes out clean. Fully cool before cutting into squares.

Chocolate Almond Tortes ⚜

2 eggs, beaten
½ c. butter, softened

1 c. sugar
1 c. flour

1 tsp. almond extract

Topping:
    1 c. pretzels, crushed
    ½ c. slivered almonds

¼ tbsp. sugar
½ c. butter, melted

2 c. semisweet chocolate chips

Preheat oven to 350°. Spray mini 2-inch wide muffin pans with cooking spray. Beat eggs in a medium-size mixing bowl. Add butter, sugar, flour and almond extract. Gently stir until combined. Fill muffin cups half full.

Combine crushed pretzels, slivered almonds and sugar together in a small mixing bowl. Pour melted butter over mixture and blend well. Sprinkle pretzel topping over the batter in each muffin cup and press topping lightly into batter.

Bake for 8 to 10 minutes or until edges are golden and toothpick inserted in the center comes out clean. Remove from oven and immediately top each torte with a tablespoon of chocolate chips. Allow chocolate to melt before swirling. Let cool and remove tortes from muffin pans.

Cinnamon Shortbread Sticks ⚜

1 ½ c. sliced almonds	2 tsp. baking powder	4 egg yolks
⅔ c. butter, softened	2 tsp. ground cinnamon	1 tsp. pure vanilla extract
1 c. sugar	1 tsp. kosher salt	4 ½ c. flour

Preheat oven to 350°. Spread sliced almonds on a jelly roll pan and toast in oven for 10 to 12 minutes or until golden brown. Remove almonds from oven and when cool, chop into very small pieces.

In a mixing bowl, beat butter on high for 30 seconds with an electric mixer. Add sugar and beat for an additional 15 seconds.

Whisk together baking powder, cinnamon and salt in a small bowl and blend with butter and sugar.

Separate the egg yolks from the whites. Add yolks and vanilla; beat well. Add flour and chopped almonds, mixing thoroughly.

Place dough on a lightly floured surface and roll out into a rectangle ½-inch thick. Cut in half, making two 3 ½-inch rectangles. Cut crosswise into 1-inch wide sticks. Place 2 inches apart on an ungreased jelly roll pan and bake for 8 to 10 minutes or until golden. Remove from oven and let cool.

Chocolate Dipping Frosting ⚜

²/₃ c. red-hot candies

1 c. white chocolate chips

1 tbsp. shortening

Chop red-hot candies into small pieces and place in a shallow bowl. Melt chocolate chips in a glass bowl in the microwave. Heat for 20 seconds at a time, stirring between, until completely melted. Do not overcook. Add shortening to melted chocolate and stir until smooth. When cookie sticks are cool, frost the tops with white chocolate and dip into crushed red-hot candies. Chill or allow to completely cool before serving.

No Knead Cranberry Orange Bread ⚜

6 tbsp. butter
6 tbsp. sugar
1 tsp. kosher salt
1½ c. milk

2 eggs, beaten
4 c. flour
2 tsp. instant yeast

½ c. dried cranberries
1 orange, zest
1 egg white, beaten

Sweet Glaze:
1 tbsp. butter, melted
1 c. powdered sugar
2 tbsp. milk

Combine butter, sugar and salt in a medium-size bowl. Scald milk, about 1 minute in the microwave. Add scalding milk to mixture, when lukewarm add beaten eggs, flour and instant yeast. Stir by hand vigorously for about 1 minute.

Rinse and dry orange before removing zest. Continue stirring and add cranberries and zest. Cover and refrigerate for 1 to 2 hours.

Prepare a jelly roll pan with cooking spray and set aside. Shape dough into braids by dividing dough in half; divide each half into 3 pieces. Roll each piece to make a long rope about 15-inches long. Braid the ropes and tuck the ends underneath. Place both braids of dough on prepared pan. Let rise 1 hour or until dough has doubled in size. Brush with beaten egg white.

Preheat oven at 350°. Bake bread for 20 to 25 minutes or until golden brown. Prepare Sweet Glaze by melting butter and whisking together melted butter, powdered sugar and milk. Brush braided bread loaves fresh out of the oven with Sweet Glaze. Serve warm. Makes 2 medium braid loaves.

Brown Butter Oatmeal Soda Bread ⚜

¼ c. butter
3 ½ c. flour
½ c. + 2 tbsp. old-fashioned oats, divided
1 tbsp. sugar
1 tbsp. fresh rosemary, chopped
2 tsp. baking powder

1 tsp. baking soda
1 tsp. kosher salt
1 tsp. coarse black pepper, divided
1 ¾ c. buttermilk
1 egg white, beaten

Preheat oven to 375° and position baking rack in center of oven. Melt butter in a small saucepan over medium heat until golden brown, about 3 minutes. Remove from heat and set aside. Combine flour, ½ cup oats, sugar, rosemary, baking powder, baking soda, salt and ¾ teaspoon pepper in large bowl and blend. Pour buttermilk and browned butter over flour mixture; stir with a fork until flour mixture is moistened.

Turn dough out onto floured surface and gently knead until dough comes together, about 7 turns. Divide dough in half and shape each half into a ball.

Stretch each ball and flatten into long ovals and place on an ungreased baking sheet 5 inches apart. Brush tops with beaten egg white and sprinkle with remaining ¼ teaspoon pepper and 2 tablespoons of oats.

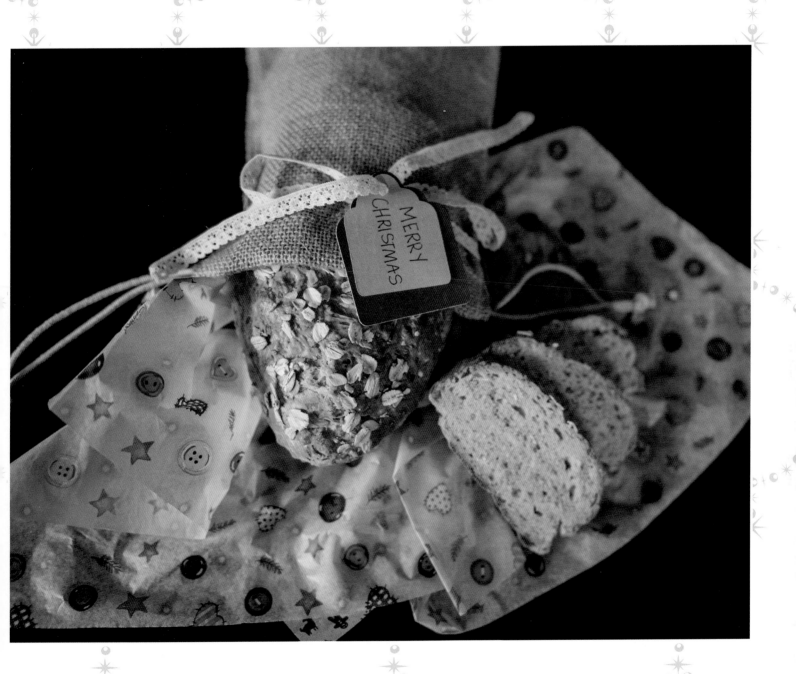

Bake bread until deep golden brown or when toothpick inserted in the center comes out clean, about 40 to 45 minutes. Cool bread loaves on rack and serve warm or at room temperature. Makes 2 loaves.

Spinach Salad in a Jar ⚜

16 oz. bag baby spinach
2 c. pomegranate seeds
1 ½ c. pine nuts
1 c. crumbled bleu cheese

Assemble salad in a large jar. Start with a layer of spinach on the bottom. Add layers of pomegranate seeds and pine nuts. Top with a layer of bleu cheese. Cover salad with lid and refrigerate.

Red Wine Vinegar Dressing ⚜

½ red onion
⅓ c. red wine vinegar
2 tbsp. Dijon mustard

1 tbsp. sugar
½ tsp. kosher salt

½ tsp. coarse black pepper
2 tbsp. olive oil

Peel and chop onion into small pieces and place in blender. Add vinegar, mustard, sugar, salt, pepper and olive oil. Mix well and chill before serving.

Southwest Salad in a Jar ⚜

1 15 oz. can black beans
6 green onion, sliced
2 c. frozen corn

3 tomatoes, diced
2 heads hearts of romaine
1 bundle fresh cilantro

2 c. shredded cheddar cheese
1 pkg. favorite corn chips

Drain and rinse black beans. Place in the bottom of a large jar. Layer sliced green onions on top of beans. Add layers of frozen corn and diced tomatoes. Rinse, chop and spin or pat dry the romaine. Add on top of tomatoes. Rinse, dry and chop cilantro and place over romaine layer. Complete salad with shredded cheddar cheese. Cover salad with lid and refrigerate. Serve with crushed corn chips and Spicy Ranch Dressing.

Spicy Ranch Dressing ⚜

1 c. buttermilk
1 c. mayonnaise
1 tsp. crushed red chili pepper
1 pkg. ranch dressing mix
1 tsp. sugar

Mix all ingredients together and chill before serving.

Asian Salad in a Jar ⚜

1 c. sliced almonds
½ c. sesame seeds
2 c. vegetable oil, for cooking
6 oz. pkg. uncooked Won Ton wraps
2 sm. heads Napa cabbage
1 ½ c. shredded carrots
8 oz. bag snow peas

Preheat oven to 350°. Toast almonds and sesame seeds for 12 to 15 minutes or until golden brown. When completely cooled, place toasted almonds and sesame seeds in the bottom of a large jar. Heat oil in a stockpot over medium heat. Cut Won Ton wraps into ¼-inch strips. Fry the strips in hot oil until golden brown. Remove with tongs and let cool on paper towel lined tray.

Cut off end of the Napa cabbage, rinse and chop; pat dry and layer on top of almonds and sesame seeds. Add layers of shredded carrots and snow peas. Top with the fried Won Ton strips. Cover salad with lid and refrigerate.

Ginger Rice Vinegar Dressing ⚜

1 tsp. fresh ginger
½ c. rice vinegar
¼ c. white wine vinegar

½ c. vegetable oil
1 tsp. sesame oil
½ c. sugar

½ tsp. kosher salt
½ tsp. coarse black pepper

Peel and mince fresh ginger. Mix all ingredients in a blender and chill before serving.

Tortellini Salad in a Jar ⚜

1 20 oz. pkg. refrigerated three cheese tortellini
1 6 oz. can whole pitted black olive
1 bundle fresh basil leaves
½ red onion
2 c. shredded mozzarella cheese
1 lb. sliced deli salami

Prepare tortellini according to directions on package. Drain, rinse and chill. Place the tortellini in the bottom of a large jar. Rinse basil and remove leaves from stems. Layer black olives and fresh basil leaves on top of tortellini. Peel and slice red onion crosswise and separate slices into rings. Add a layer of onions and a layer of shredded mozzarella cheese. Slice salami into thin strips and place on top. Cover salad with lid and refrigerate.

Balsamic Vinaigrette Dressing ⚜

⅓ c. balsamic vinegar
2 tbsp. red wine vinegar
2 tsp. Dijon mustard
2 tsp. Italian spices

¾ c. olive oil
½ tsp. kosher salt
½ tsp. coarse black pepper

Mix all ingredients in a blender and chill before serving.

CHAPTER EIGHT

The Stroke of Twelve

Make the excitement happen with these party-perfect dishes mixed with merriment and cheer! Each recipe is easy to bring to any midnight gathering. This harmony of flavors will help you celebrate and ring in the New Year.

The time is right for a fun filled informal buffet. The kitchen setting makes it effortless to mingle and enjoy the moment. As the clock ticks... the countdown begins... enjoy this generous buffet and satisfy your sweet tooth as the laughter never ends.

Pomegranate Orange Salad ⚜

2 heads hearts of romaine
6 ripe avocados

8 tangerines
1 lime

1 ½ c. pomegranate seeds

Clean and chop romaine; chill. Slice and remove pits from avocados; cut into chunks. Cut lime in half and squeeze juice over avocados to keep from turing brown. Peel and break apart tangerines. Lightly toss romaine, avocado chunks, tangerines and pomegranate seeds in a large serving bowl. Drizzle with Champagne Vinaigrette Dressing.

Serving pieces from Napa Home & Garden

Champagne Vinaigrette Dressing ⚜

½ c. champagne vinegar
2 tsp. Dijon mustard
½ tsp. minced garlic
½ tsp. parsley flakes

2 tbsp. fresh lemon juice
½ tsp. coarse black pepper
4 tbsp. olive oil

Serving pieces from Napa Home & Garden

In a small bowl or glass jar, add all the ingredients except the olive oil and mix well. Slowly add olive oil, whisking together. Refrigerate until ready to serve. Serve over Pomegranate Orange Salad.

Garlic Veggie Dip ⚜

1 ½ c. sour cream
1 tsp. garlic pepper

½ tsp. coarse black pepper
½ tsp. kosher salt

2 tsp. minced dried onion
½ tsp. garlic salt

Whisk sour cream and all seasonings in a bowl. Chill dip before serving.

Veggie Tray ⚜

2 red bell peppers
2 yellow bell peppers
2 c. fresh sugar snap peas

Clean all the vegetables; seed bell peppers and cut into thin strips. Place on serving dish with Garlic Veggie Dip.

Sesame Chicken Poppers ⚜

2 c. cooked shredded chicken
2 tbsp. rice vinegar
4 oz. cream cheese
1 tsp. soy sauce
½ tsp. sesame oil
½ tsp. kosher salt

½ tsp. coarse black pepper
1 tbsp. fresh ginger, peeled & grated
¼ c. toasted sesame seeds
1 pkg. square Won Ton wrappers
1 qt. vegetable oil for frying
coarse sea salt, garnish

Place shredded chicken in a medium-size mixing bowl and drizzle with vinegar. Combine cream cheese, soy sauce, sesame oil, salt, pepper and grated ginger. Blend chicken with cream cheese mixture and fold in toasted sesame seeds.

Place 1 teaspoon of chicken filling in the center of a Won Ton wrapper. Dip fingers in water and run wet fingers along all edges of the Won Ton wrapper. Fold Won Ton, pulling all corners into the center and pressing firmly together (as pictured). Repeat.

Heat oil in heavy stockpot over medium-high heat. Fry Won Tons in small batches until brown and crispy, turning twice. Drain on paper towel lined trays and sprinkle with coarse sea salt.

Helpful Hint: Use the same quart of vegetable oil for both popper recipes.

Cheddar Jalapeño Poppers ⚜

3 jalapenos
1 8 oz. pkg. cream cheese

1 c. shredded cheddar cheese
1 pkg. square Won Ton wrappers

1 qt. vegetable oil for frying
coarse sea salt for garnish

Clean, seed and mince jalapenos. Combine cream cheese, cheddar cheese and jalapenos in a small mixing bowl. Place 1 teaspoon of cream cheese filling in the center of a Won Ton wrapper. Dip fingers in water and run wet fingers along all edges of the Won Ton wrapper. Fold Won Ton, pulling all corners into the center and pressing firmly together (as pictured). Repeat.

Heat oil in a heavy stockpot over medium-high heat. Fry Won Tons in small batches until brown and crispy, turning twice. Drain on paper towel lined trays and sprinkle with coarse sea salt.

Shrimp Endive Boats ⚜

2 sm. heads endive
2 c. deveined cooked shrimp
6 celery stalks
1 tbsp. fresh dill
1 fresh lime, juice
kosher salt and coarse black pepper to taste

Cut off ends of the endive heads and separate leaves; rinse and pat dry. Before filling, chill endive until crisp.
Cut shrimp into small pieces and put in medium-size bowl. Rinse and dice celery and mince fresh dill. Add celery and dill to shrimp. Toss with fresh squeezed lime juice, salt and pepper. Spoon shrimp mixture onto endive leaves. Chill before serving.

Serving pieces from Napa Home & Garden

Pear & Gorgonzola Endive Boats ⚜

2 ripe yellow Bartlett pears
1 tbsp. champagne vinegar

½ tsp. coarse black pepper
1 tbsp. honey

2 heads endive
3 oz. crumbled Gorgonzola cheese

Clean, core and cut pears into small chunks. Whisk vinegar, pepper and honey together and toss over pears. Cut off ends of the endive heads and separate leaves; rinse and pat dry. Before filling, chill leaves until crisp. Spoon pear mixture onto endive leaves and sprinkle with Gorgonzola cheese. Chill until serving.

Ribeye Tostadas ⚜

16 oz. ribeye steak
3 cloves garlic
¼ c. lime juice

1 tbsp. chili powder
¼ tsp. cumin

1 tsp. kosher salt
½ tsp. garlic pepper

Slice ribeye steaks in thin slices. Peel and mince garlic cloves. In a Ziploc™ bag combine lime juice, garlic, chili powder, cumin, kosher salt and garlic pepper; mix well. Add steak slices to marinade. Marinate for 1 hour. Remove steaks from bag and discard marinade.

1 tbsp. olive oil
1 green bell pepper
1 yellow onion
1 c. cherry tomatoes

Heat olive oil in grill pan over medium-high heat. Clean and seed pepper; cut into long thin slices. Peel and slice onion in half; cut into thin slices. Clean and slice cherry tomatoes in half.

When oil is hot, add steak slices and grill for 2 to 3 minutes. Add vegetables and cook an additional 2 to 3 minutes. Place grilled steak and vegetables with desired garnishes on cheese tostadas. Serve immediately.

Cheese Corn Crisps ⚜

12 flat corn tostadas
1 ½ c. shredded cheddar cheese

Preheat oven to broil. Spread cheese on tostadas and broil for 1 to 2 minutes or until cheese is melted. Remove from oven and set aside.

Garnishes:

    ½ c. favorite salsa
    ½ c. guacamole
    ½ c. sour cream

Cilantro Fish Tacos ⚜

1 tsp. olive oil	1 lb. skinned salmon	1 c. cherry tomatoes, sliced
½ tsp. coarse black pepper	1 lime, fresh juice	½ c. chopped fresh cilantro
1 lb. skinned Dover sole fillet	12-15 fresh corn tortillas, heated	Confetti Broccoli Slaw

Place olive oil and pepper in skillet over medium high heat. Cut sole and salmon into chunks and place in hot skillet. Cook 3 to 4 minutes turning occasionally until fully cooked. Remove from heat and squeeze lime juice over fish.

Assemble tacos by placing warm, fish pieces on each heated tortilla and topping with Confetti Broccoli Slaw, tomatoes, and chopped cilantro.

Confetti Broccoli Slaw ⚜

1 c. mayonnaise
1 c. sour cream
1 tbsp. lemon juice
1 tsp. honey
2 tsp. olive oil
12 oz. pkg. broccoli slaw
2 tbsp. fresh flat parsley, chopped
2 carrots, peel, julienne
½ red onion, peel, julienne

¼ tsp. kosher salt
¼ tsp. coarse black pepper

Combine mayonnaise, sour cream, lemon juice, honey and olive oil; whisk together until well combined.

When ready to serve, toss vegetables with dressing and finish with salt and pepper. Serve as topping for Cilantro Fish Tacos.

candles by Vance Kitira – vancekitira.com

Green Chili Soup

2 lbs. chicken tenders
3 lb. bag Yukon gold potatoes, diced
¼ c. butter
1 lg. white onion
½ c. flour
1-2 qts. chicken broth
    (from granulated chicken bouillon)
12 oz. bag frozen corn
1 7 oz. can diced green chilies
1 tsp. coarse black pepper
4 c. shredded cheddar cheese
1 lg. red bell pepper
1 lg. yellow bell pepper
1 qt. heavy whipping cream
1 c. chopped fresh cilantro, garnish

Spray medium-size stockpot with cooking spray. Place frozen chicken tenders in pot on medium-high heat and cover with lid. Let cook, stirring occasionally until the chicken is completely cooked, about 10 to 12 minutes. When chicken is fully cooked, drain and pull chicken apart with forks into bite-size pieces.

Clean, peel and dice potatoes; boil in a pot of salted water until tender. Drain and set aside.

In a large stockpot melt butter. Peel and dice onion. Add to melted butter and sauté for 2 to 4 minutes. When onions become clear, whisk in flour and cook for 1 to 2 minutes. Whisk in 1 quart of broth and stir until thickened. Add corn, green chilies and pepper. Fold in shredded chicken, cooked potatoes and shredded cheese. Bring to a low simmer.

Clean, seed and dice bell peppers; fold into soup. Stir while adding cream. Add additional broth for desired thickness. Heat thoroughly. Top each serving with fresh cilantro and serve.

candles by Vance Kitira – vancekitira.com

Fire Crackers ⚜

1 ⅓ c. vegetable oil
1 tbsp. red pepper flakes
1 pkg. ranch dressing mix

1 tsp. garlic pepper
2 tbsp. lemon pepper

1 tsp. kosher salt
1 11 oz. box mini saltine crackers

Mix vegetable oil and seasonings together. Place 1 box of mini saltines in a large Ziploc™ bag. Pour the seasoned oil over the crackers. Toss until seasonings are absorbed; let sit in bag for 2 to 3 hours before serving.

Salted Caramel Brownies ⚜

1 c. butter
14 oz. semisweet chocolate chips, divided
3 oz. unsweetened baking chocolate
3 eggs
1 tsp. pure vanilla extract
1 c. sugar
½ c. + 2 tbsp. flour, divided
1 ½ tsp. baking powder
½ tsp. kosher salt
5 to 6 oz. jar caramel sauce
2-3 tsp. flaked sea salt

Preheat oven to 350°. Prepare a 9 x 13 baking dish with cooking spray. Set a medium-size glass bowl over a pan of simmering water. In the bowl, stir the butter, 8 ounces chocolate chips and the unsweetened baking chocolate until melted. Cool for 15 minutes. In a large mixing bowl, whisk together eggs, vanilla and sugar. Add the chocolate mixture into the egg mixture and cool to room temperature.

In a medium bowl, combine ½ cup of flour, baking powder, and salt. Stir and add to the chocolate mixture. In another bowl, toss the remaining 6 ounces of chocolate chips with the remaining 2 tablespoons of flour and add to the chocolate mixture. Spread evenly in the prepared pan.

Bake for 35 minutes or until a toothpick comes out clean. As soon as the brownies are removed from oven, place the jar of caramel sauce, without the lid, in microwave and heat until caramel is smooth and pourable. Stir and drizzle the caramel evenly over hot brownies and sprinkle with the sea salt. Cool completely and cut into bars.

Coconut Doughnut Holes ⚜

1/3 c. milk

1/3 c. boiling water

1 tbsp. active dry yeast

3 1/2 c. flour

1/3 c. sugar

1/4 tsp. kosher salt

1/3 c. butter, softened

2 eggs, whisked

1 qt. vegetable oil for frying

Glaze:

1/3 c. water

1 tbsp. pure vanilla extract

6 c. powdered sugar

2 c. sweetened flake coconut

In a small measuring bowl, combine milk and boiling water. Add yeast and gently stir; set aside for 5 minutes until bubbly. In a large mixing bowl, combine flour, sugar and salt. Cut in the butter using a pastry blender until it resembles pea-sized crumbs. Add eggs and yeast mixture to the flour and stir, about 5 minutes, until smooth dough forms.

Turn dough out onto a lightly floured surface and knead with hands about 5 to 10 minutes, until dough is springy and little bubbles form on the surface. Place dough back in bowl; cover with plastic wrap and let rise 1 hour or until double in size.

Once raised, cut dough into 4 equal pieces. Roll out each piece into a long rope about 1½-inches thick. Cut strips about 1-inch long and roll into a ball. Place on pan and cover doughnut holes.

Prepare glaze. Mix water, vanilla and powdered sugar together in a medium-size bowl. Set aside while frying.

Heat oil in a large pot over medium-high heat. Place doughnut holes into hot oil, turning until golden on both sides, about 1 to 2 minutes. Only fry a few at a time so they will not stick together. Remove doughnut holes from oil and place on a jelly roll pan lined with paper towels to absorb oil. Dip doughnut holes in Glaze while still warm and immediately roll in coconut. Serve.

Sugar Cookie Fruit Pizzas ⚜

½ c. butter, softened
½ c. shortening
½ c. sugar
½ c. powdered sugar

1 egg
1 tsp. almond extract
2 ¼ c. flour

½ tsp. cream of tartar
½ tsp. baking soda
½ tsp. kosher salt

Preheat oven to 350°. Blend butter, shortening and both sugars together until creamy. Add egg and almond extract. In a separate bowl, whisk all dry ingredients together. Combine with butter mixture and blend well. Roll out dough ¼-inch thick and cut into circles with a circle cookie cutter. Place cookies on jelly roll pan sprayed with cooking spray. Bake for 6 to 8 minutes. Place the cookies on a rack to cool.

Almond Butter Cream Frosting ⚜

6 oz. cream cheese
1 c. butter, softened
1 tsp. almond extract
4 c. powdered sugar

Place cream cheese and butter in a bowl. Using an electric mixer beat for 2 to 3 minutes. Add almond extract and powdered sugar. Whip until light and fluffy.

Garnishes:
    4 kiwis
    2 c. fresh blackberries
    2 c. fresh strawberries
    1 c. fresh blueberries

Rinse fruit, slice strawberries, rinse, peel and slice kiwis. Frost cookies; arrange kiwis, blackberries, strawberries and blueberries on top of each cookie (as pictured).

Fudge Brownies ⚜

1 c. butter, softened
½ c. unsweetened cocoa powder
2 c. flour
2 c. sugar
4 eggs, whisked
1 ½ tbsp. pure vanilla extract

Preheat oven to 350°. Prepare a 9 x 13 baking dish with cooking spray. Combine all brownie ingredients in a bowl and blend gently with a fork, until combined.

Pour batter into baking dish and bake for 20 to 25 minutes. Remove brownies from oven and cool 10 minutes. Frost while still warm.

Fudge Frosting ⚜

¼ c. butter, softened
½ c. milk
¼ c. unsweetened cocoa powder

3 c. powdered sugar
⅛ tsp. kosher salt

Combine butter, milk, cocoa, powdered sugar and salt together in a small mixing bowl and beat with an electric mixer until smooth. Frost the warm brownies. Cool completely before cutting into squares. Serve.

White Chocolate Raspberry Bar ⚜

1 16.5 oz. roll refrigerated sugar cookie dough

3 4 oz. white chocolate baking bars, divided

12 oz. jar raspberry jam

Heat oven to 350°. In a greased 9 x 13 pan, break up cookie dough. Press dough evenly in bottom of pan to form crust. Chop one 4 oz. chocolate baking bar and sprinkle over crust; press firmly into dough. Bake 16 to 20 minutes or until light golden brown. Remove crust from oven.

Spread jam evenly over crust. Return to oven; bake 10 minutes longer. Cool completely. Chop remaining white chocolate baking bars. Sprinkle over jam on baked cookie crust and allow to fully cool before cutting into small squares.

Details...

A medley of teal colored tapered candles are bound together with silver wired tinsel placed on small silver and white saucers.

candles by Vance Kitira - vancekitira.com

Notes & Comments

_____

_____

_____

_____

_____

_____

_____

_____

_____

_____

_____

_____

_____

_____

_____

_____

_____

A Quiet Celebration

As another year comes to a close, an invitation to a quiet celebration is a welcoming end to the holiday season. We pause and take time to reflect, make hopeful resolutions… promising this year to keep them. With this year-end celebration we begin anew.

This Winter White Cauliflower Soup served with a hearty Steak & Gorgonzola Salad, Rosemary Cheese Pastry and Lemon Cheesecake Tartlets is the perfect way to ring in the New Year.

Steak & Gorgonzola Salad ⚜

2 heads hearts of romaine
10 oz. bag spring mix

1 8 oz. pkg. Gorgonzola cheese
candied pecans

grilled ribeye steaks
Grey Poupon™ Dressing

Clean and chop lettuce into bite-size pieces and chill. When ready to serve, combine romaine and spring mix on a serving tray. Coarsely crumble Gorgonzola cheese over lettuce. Top with thin steak strips and Candied Pecans. Drizzle Grey Poupon™ Dressing over salad and serve.

Steak Marinade:

    3 lbs. ribeye steaks
    4 tbsp. olive oil
    3 tbsp. balsamic vinegar
    3 tbsp. rice vinegar
    ½ tsp. onion salt
    ½ tsp. cayenne pepper
    ⅛ tsp. red chili flakes
    1 tsp. kosher salt
    ½ tsp. coarse black pepper

With a fork poke holes in each ribeye so the steaks will absorb the marinade.

In a bowl whisk all remaining ingredients together. Put marinade and steaks into a Ziploc™ bag and marinate for 1 to 3 hours.

Grilling:

marinated steaks

½ tsp. kosher salt

2 tbsp. olive oil

½ tsp. coarse black pepper

Heat a grill pan over medium-high heat and drizzle with olive oil. Place steaks on hot grill pan and sprinkle with salt and pepper. Cook to desired doneness. Cut into thin strips to serve on salad.

Candied Pecans:

⅓ c. butter

2 c. pecans halves

⅔ c. brown sugar

½ tsp. kosher salt

Preheat oven to 425°. In a heavy skillet, melt butter over medium heat. Add brown sugar and mix well. Fold in pecans and coat evenly. Remove skillet off heat and spread out coated pecans on a jelly roll pan; roast in oven for 10 to 12 minutes. Remove pecans from oven and sprinkle with salt. Let cool completely before chopping Candied Pecans.

Grey Poupon™ Dressing ⚜

2 tbsp. Grey Poupon™ mustard
½ c. rice vinegar
½ c. white wine vinegar
½ c. sugar
½ c. vegetable oil
1 tsp. coarse black pepper

Place all ingredients in blender and mix well. Chill before serving.

Cucumber Cream Cheese Boats ⚜

| 8 sm. cucumbers | 1 tsp. fresh dill | ½ c. cottage cheese |
| 4 celery stalks | 4 oz. cream cheese, softened | 1 tsp. garlic pepper |

Clean and cut cucumbers in half. Using a small spoon remove center seeds of cucumbers, leaving the shell (as pictured). Clean and chop celery into small pieces. Mince fresh dill. In a small mixing bowl, combine cream cheese, cottage cheese, celery, dill and garlic pepper. Fill each cucumber boat with cream cheese spread and chill before serving.

Winter White Cauliflower Soup ⚜

2 heads cauliflower
1 red onion
8 celery stalks
6 cloves garlic
4 tbsp. olive oil

1 ½ tsp. kosher salt
½ c. butter
²⁄₃ c. flour
2 tsp. dried rosemary

1 tsp. dried thyme
4 c. heavy whipping cream
4 to 6 c. chicken broth
4 green onions, for garnish

Preheat oven to 425°. Clean and core each cauliflower head; chop into small pieces. Peel and chop red onion. Clean and dice celery. Peel and crush garlic cloves with a garlic press. Whisk together garlic, olive oil and salt; toss over cauliflower, onion and celery. Spread out on 2 jelly roll pans and roast in the oven for 15 to 20 minutes or until edges of the cauliflower are golden brown.

In a large stockpot, melt butter and fold in flour, rosemary and thyme. Cook for 2 to 3 minutes until golden brown. Slowly fold in cream and 4 cups chicken broth.

Add roasted vegetables and bring to a low simmer. If soup is too thick add more chicken broth. Garnish with chopped green onions and serve.

Rosemary Cheese Pastry ⚜

1 17.3 oz. pkg. frozen puff pastry, 2 sheets
1 egg white
1 white onion
2 tbsp. olive oil
¼ tsp. kosher salt

¼ tsp. coarse black pepper
1 8 oz. bell pepper goat cheese
½ tsp. dried rosemary
balsamic vinegar, garnish

Thaw puff pastry package in refrigerator. Preheat oven to 400°. Spread out thawed puff pastry sheets on jelly roll pan and brush with egg white. Bake for 7 minutes.

Peel and slice onion. Heat olive oil in a skillet over medium-high heat. When oil is hot, add onion slices, salt and pepper. Stir onions while cooking for 2 to 3 minutes.

Arrange onion slices and scatter ¼ teaspoon-size scoops of goat cheese over each puff pastry. Top with rosemary and bake 5 to 7 minutes or until golden brown. Serve with your favorite balsamic.

Helpful Hint: If making this entire meal for a gathering, set aside egg yolk from this recipe use for the Lemon Cheesecake Tartlets.

Lemon Cheesecake Tartlets ⚜

Lemon Crust:

½ c. butter, softened	½ tsp. pure vanilla extract	1 tsp. lemon zest, finely grated
3 tbsp. sugar	1 c. flour	½ tsp. kosher salt
2 egg yolks	1 c. graham cracker crumbs	

Cream Cheese Filling:

8 oz. cream cheese, softened	1 egg	1 tbsp. fresh lemon juice
1 c. powdered sugar	2 tbsp. lemon zest, finely grated	½ tsp. pure vanilla extract

Tart Lemon Topping:

1 ¾ c. water	¼ tsp. kosher salt	4 egg yolks
1 ¾ c. sugar	1 lemon, zest	1 tbsp. butter
5 tbsp. cornstarch	⅓ c. fresh lemon juice	

1 can Reddi Whip™, garnish

Preheat oven to 350°. In a medium-size mixing bowl, cream together butter, sugar, egg yolks and vanilla with an electric mixer. Add flour, graham cracker crumbs, zest and salt. Prepare 24 muffin cups with cooking spray and press crust into each cup, pressing firmly on bottom and sides. Set aside.

Combine all Cream Cheese Filling ingredients together in a mixing bowl and blend well with an electric mixer. Pour cheesecake filling into each Lemon Crust cup and bake for 15 to 18 minutes or until center of cheesecake is set.

Prepare Tart Lemon Topping while cheesecakes are baking. Heat water in a small saucepan. In a separate bowl, blend sugar, cornstarch, salt and zest. When water begins to boil, add sugar mixture and whisk while cooking until liquid is clear. Add lemon juice and egg yolks. Cook for 1 additional minute, stirring constantly. Fold in butter and stir until melted. Chill in refrigerator.

Top each cheesecake with Tart Lemon Topping and chill. Just before serving garnish with Reddi Whip™.

Helpful Hint: If making this entire meal for a gathering, set aside egg white from this recipe to use for the Rosemary Goat Cheese Puff Pastry.

candles by Mixture - mixtureusa.com

candles by Mixture – mixtureusa.com

Details…

Silver chargers with plain white dishes are simple and elegant. Adding a touch of gray with simple soup bowls sitting on gray salad plates coordinate with our signature paper placemats and napkins. Soft pink long stemmed glasses are an graceful touch.

Details…

White candles in clear glass containers accent the pink ceramic flowers that are the perfect subtle touch for this Quiet Celebration.

Notes & Comments

_____

_____

_____

_____

_____

_____

_____

_____

_____

_____

_____

_____

_____

_____

_____

_____

_____

Shopping List

Each recipe is designed to serve eight to ten

3 lbs. ribeye steaks
1 8 oz. pkg. Gorgonzola cheese
1 8 oz. bell pepper goat cheese
½ c. cottage cheese
4 c. heavy whipping cream
1 lb. butter
12 oz. cream cheese
1 can Reddi Whip™
1 17.3 oz. pkg. frozen puff
pastry
2 heads hearts of romaine
10 oz. bag spring mix

2 heads cauliflower
1 red onion
1 white onion
4 green onions
12 celery stalks
6 cloves garlic
8 sm. cucumbers
1 tsp. fresh dill
4 lemons
½ tsp. cayenne pepper
⅛ tsp. red chili flakes
2 ½ tsp. dried rosemary

1 tsp. dried thyme
1 tsp. garlic pepper
5 tbsp. cornstarch
¼ c. balsamic vinegar
¾ c. rice vinegar
½ c. white wine vinegar
2 tbsp. Grey Poupon™ mustard
6 c. chicken broth
2 c. pecans halves
1 c. graham cracker crumbs

Staples:

flour
pure vanilla extract
sugar
powdered sugar

brown sugar
eggs
vegetable oil
olive oil

kosher salt
onion salt
coarse black pepper

shopping lists available for print online.

Be Mine, Valentine

On this day of hearts, prepare a memorable menu with an intimate setting. Heartfelt dining at home with sweetheart couples is a romantic twist to this Valentine's evening. We chose to emphasize a heart-themed gathering to enhance the expressions of the day.

Sweet sentiments create happy hearts while sharing these cherished moments with guests is sure to endear. This nontraditional celebration of Valentine's Day with couples can become an enduring gathering with heart.

Savory Pita Hearts ⚜

4 whole-wheat pita pockets
12 slices precooked bacon
1 c. shredded mozzarella cheese

1 c. cottage cheese
1 tsp. kosher salt

2 tsp. olive oil
fresh dill, for garnish

Cut pita pockets into heart shapes with a small heart cookie cutter (half of a pita pocket should yield 4 small hearts when pitas are separated). Cut precooked bacon into tiny bits with kitchen scissors and set aside. Combine mozzarella and cottage cheese together. Fold in salt.

Heat olive oil in a large frying pan. Make sandwiches by placing cheese mixture and bacon between two heart-shaped pita bread slices. Lightly toast each side in frying pan until golden brown and cheese melts. Garnish with fresh dill and serve.

Shrimp Avocado Salad ⚜

1 head hearts of romaine
1 ½ c. celery
6 sm. avocados
4 limes
3 c. lg. cooked shrimp
1 tbsp. fresh dill, chopped
10 oz. bag baby spinach

Clean, rinse and chop romaine. Clean and dice celery. Cut avocados in half and remove pit; peel and slice into bite-size pieces. Cut limes in half. Squeeze juice of 2 limes over the avocado to keep from turning brown.

Cut the large shrimp into small bite-size pieces. Squeeze juice of the remaining limes over shrimp. Combine all ingredients in a serving bowl and toss with Italian Vinaigrette.

Italian Vinaigrette ⚜

1 c. rice vinegar
1 tsp. Italian seasoning

¼ c. sugar
⅓ c. vegetable oil

Mix all ingredients together and chill before tossing salad with vinaigrette.

Grilled Carrots & Zucchini ⚜

8 lg. carrots

6 sm. zucchini

2 tbsp. olive oil

1 tsp. kosher salt

½ tsp. onion salt

½ tsp. coarse black pepper

Peel and rinse carrots. Cut into thin slices lengthwise. Clean and cut the ends off of each zucchini; cut in long, wide slices (as pictured).

Using a grill pan, heat olive oil, salts and pepper over medium- high heat. Place sliced vegetables on grill pan and cook, turning 3 to 4 times. Cook vegetables 2 to 3 minutes until tender but crisp. Serve.

Marinara Sauce ⚜

10 Roma tomatoes
2 tbsp. butter
2 tbsp. olive oil
1 tsp. coarse black pepper
½ tsp. garlic salt
½ tsp. Italian seasoning
3 tbsp. sugar
1 c. tomato sauce

Rinse and chop tomatoes into small chunks. Combine butter and olive oil in skillet over medium heat. Add tomatoes, pepper, garlic salt, Italian seasoning and sugar. Simmer for 30 minutes, stirring occasionally. Fold in tomato sauce and simmer for 2 to 3 minutes.

Marinated Red Onions ⚜

1 med. red onion
½ c. white vinegar
¼ c. vegetable oil
½ tsp. garlic pepper

2 tbsp. sugar
¼ tsp. dried oregano
¼ tsp. kosher salt

Peel and slice onion into thin rings. Whisk all other ingredients together. Add onions to seasoned oil and vinegar. Marinate in refrigerator at least an hour before serving. Garnish Lemon Pepper Chicken Strips with chilled Marinated Red Onions.

Garlic Mashed Potatoes ⚜

3 ½ lbs. russet potatoes
2 tbsp. kosher salt
6 cloves garlic
½ c. butter, melted
1 ½-2 c. half-and-half, heated
¾ c. fresh shredded Parmesan cheese

Peel and cut potatoes in fourths. Place in a large stockpot. Add salt and cover with water. Bring to a boil over medium-high heat and then reduce heat to maintain a rolling boil. Cook until potatoes are tender when poked with a fork.

Peel and crush garlic. Heat the half-and-half and garlic in a saucepan over medium heat until it begins to simmer. Remove from heat and set aside.

When potatoes are cooked, drain off the water. Add melted butter and 1 ½ cups hot half-and-half gradually over potatoes and mix with an electric mixer. Add remaining half-and-half for desired consistency. Fold in Parmesan cheese and garnish with coarse black pepper. Serve.

Lemon Pepper Chicken Strips ⚜

6 boneless, skinless chicken breasts
3 eggs
1 tsp. kosher salt

½ tsp. coarse black pepper
1 c. crushed Club Crackers™
3 tbsp. flour

4 tbsp. lemon pepper
2 c. vegetable oil, for cooking
fresh basil, for garnish

Rinse and pat dry chicken breasts. Cut into diagonal strips (as pictured). In a shallow bowl beat eggs, salt and black pepper together. In a Ziploc™ bag crush crackers. Place the crackers and flour in a separate shallow pie dish; stir in lemon pepper and mix well.

Heat vegetable oil in a heavy stockpot. Dip each chicken strip into beaten eggs and coat evenly with crushed crackers.

When oil is hot and pops, place chicken strips in hot oil; while cooking turn 2 or 3 times. Cook 3 minutes or until golden brown. Keep warm until ready to serve.

When ready to serve place Marinara sauce, Garlic Mashed Potatoes, Lemon Pepper Chicken Strips, garnished with Marinated Red Onions and basil on each serving dish.

Winter Berry Bread ⚜

1 ¾ c. flour
1 ½ tsp. baking powder
½ tsp. kosher salt

1 ½ c. fresh raspberries, rinsed, divided
½ c. butter, softened
¾ c. sugar

2 eggs
1 tsp. pure vanilla extract
¼ c. heavy whipping cream

Preheat oven to 350°. Prepare the bottom and sides of a 9 x 5 loaf pan with cooking spray. In a bowl, whisk together the flour, baking powder and salt. Remove 1 tablespoon of the flour mixture and place in a separate bowl; toss with ½ cup of raspberries. (This will help prevent the berries from sinking to the bottom of the pan during baking.) Set aside.

In another bowl, with a hand mixer beat the butter for about 1 minute. Add sugar and continue to beat until light and fluffy for another 2 to 3 minutes.

Mash remaining raspberries and set aside 2 tablespoons for glaze. Combine mashed raspberries with the sugar mixture. Add eggs, one at a time, beating well after each addition. Scrape down the sides of the bowl as needed. Beat in the vanilla and cream.

With the mixer on low, add the flour mixture. Mix only until combined. Gently fold in the flour-coated berries.

Pour the batter into the prepared pan and bake for about 55 to 65 minutes or until a toothpick inserted in the center comes out clean.

Raspberry Glaze

1/3 c. powdered sugar   2 tbsp. fresh raspberries, mashed

In a small microwave safe bowl, stir the sugar with mashed berries. Microwave for about 20 seconds or until sugar has dissolved.

When bread is baked, remove from loaf pan and quickly wrap hot loaf in plastic wrap to capture moisture. When loaf is cooled, top with Raspberry Glaze. Slice and serve.

White Chocolate Cheesecake ⚜

2 c. Oreo™ cookies, crushed
½ c. butter, melted
2 4 oz. Ghirardelli white chocolate baking bars
2 8 oz. pkg. cream cheese

1 c. sugar
1 tsp. pure vanilla extract
3 eggs

Preheat oven to 325°. Remove centers from cookies and place just the chocolate cookies in a large Ziploc™ bag. Crush with a rolling pin. Add melted butter to crumbs in bag and combine. Press crumbs into a 9-inch round springform pan or a flower-shaped baking mold (as pictured).

Chop white chocolate bars into chunks and place in a glass bowl. Microwave for 20 seconds at a time, stirring after each time, until the chocolate is smooth and evenly melted. Cool for 5 minutes. Combine cream cheese, sugar, vanilla and eggs in a medium-size mixing bowl and beat together with an electric mixer. Add melted chocolate and beat until well combined.

Pour cheesecake mixture over cookie crust and bake for 50 to 60 minutes or until center of cheesecake is set. Remove from oven and refrigerate until serving.

If using flower-shaped baking mold, slice into 4 equal parts to create 4 heart-shaped pieces. Serve with Sweetheart Strawberry Sauce.

Helpful Hint: Line pan with parchment paper for easy removal.

placemats and napkins available at thegatheringoffriends.com

Sweetheart Strawberry Sauce ⚜

3 c. strawberries   1 c. sugar   ¼ c. water

Rinse, remove stems and slice strawberries. Combine ingredients together in a small saucepan. Cook sauce for 15 minutes or until desired thickness is achieved. Serve over White Chocolate Cheesecake.

placemats and napkins available at thegatheringoffriends.com

Details...

This is one of our favorite meals we have ever created. The perfect blend of Italian flavors, includes sweet marinara sauce layered with Garlic Mashed Potatoes, Lemon Pepper Chicken Strips and Marinated Red Onions makes an incredible meal.

Details...

An unexpected combination of traditional red roses and candles bound tightly together with teal colored ribbon dress this welcome table.

Notes & Comments

_____
_____
_____
_____
_____
_____
_____
_____
_____
_____
_____
_____
_____
_____
_____
_____
_____
_____

Shopping List

Each recipe is designed to serve six to eight

3 c. lg. cooked shrimp
6 boneless, skinless chicken breasts
12 slices precooked bacon
2 c. half-and-half
1 c. cottage cheese
1 lb. butter
1 doz. eggs
¾ c. fresh shredded
Parmesan cheese
1 c. shredded mozzarella cheese
¼ c. heavy whipping cream
2 8 oz. pkg. cream cheese
1 head celery

6 sm. avocados
4 limes
1 bunch fresh dill
1 sm. pkg. fresh basil
10 oz. bag baby spinach
1 head hearts of romaine
3 ½ lbs. russet potatoes
6 cloves garlic
10 Roma tomatoes
1 med. red onion
8 lg. carrots
6 sm. zucchini
1 ½ c. fresh raspberries

3 c. strawberries
1 ½ tsp. Italian seasoning
4 tbsp. lemon pepper
½ tsp. garlic pepper
¼ tsp. dried oregano
4 whole-wheat pita pockets
1 c. rice vinegar
½ c. white vinegar
1 c. tomato sauce
2 4 oz. Ghirardelli white
chocolate baking bars
1 16 oz. box Club Crackers™
1 15.35 oz. pkg. Oreo™ cookies

Staples:

flour
baking powder
pure vanilla extract
sugar

powdered sugar
vegetable oil
olive oil
kosher salt

garlic salt
onion salt
coarse black pepper

shopping lists available for print online.

Easter Joy

Spring arrives quietly as earth awakens. Budding bulbs and blossoming branches bloom, bursting in beauty, giving us a promised renewal. Easter Sunday morning is a glorious occasion to gather and celebrate rebirth and newness of life.

This springtime midday meal offers an array of delicious crepes and a variety of sweet and savory fillings. Indulge in the flavors of the season with Citrus Glazed Fruit Salad, Garden Fresh Scrambled Eggs, Cheddar Garlic Potatoes and home baked Cinnamon Oatmeal Pound Cake with rich Brown Butter Frosting.

Simplicity is part of the charm of the soft pastel tablescape. Details make all the difference. Tradition never tasted so good!

Citrus Glazed Fruit Salad ⚜

2 lemons
1 c. powdered sugar
1 c. blueberries
1 c. strawberries, sliced

1 c. cantaloupe, diced
1 c. pineapple, diced
1 c. grapes

1 c. raspberries
1 c. honeydew melon, diced
8 to 10 tangerines, peeled and separated

Rinse and slice lemons in half and juice. Combine lemon juice and powdered sugar together in a small mixing bowl. Clean and slice fruit. In a large bowl, mix fruit together and toss lightly with the sugar glaze. Transfer to a serving dish. Chill before serving.

Easter Egg Cobb Salad ⚜

2 heads hearts of romaine
2 lbs. thick sliced, oven roasted deli turkey
8 hard-boiled eggs
3 avocados
1 lime
3 tomatoes

Rinse and chop hearts of romaine lettuce into bite-size pieces. Chill. Slice deli turkey into ½-inch cubes. Peel hard-boiled eggs and slice. Slice avocados in half and remove pit; peel and cut into small chunks. Rinse and slice lime in half and squeeze fresh juice over avocado and toss. Clean and slice tomatoes into 8 sections. Arrange salad ingredients in a glass bowl (as pictured). Cover and chill before serving.

Cobb Dressing ⚜

½ c. vegetable oil
1 c. rice vinegar
1 c. sugar
1 tsp. kosher salt

½ tsp. dried oregano
½ tsp. dried basil
½ tsp. onion salt
½ tsp. coarse black pepper

Combine oil, vinegar, sugar and seasonings together in a blender and mix well. Chill before serving.

Carrots & Herb Vegetable Dip ⚜

½ c. sour cream
1 c. mayonnaise
1 tsp. dill weed
1 tsp. dried tarragon leaves
1 tbsp. parsley flakes

1 tbsp. fresh chopped chives
¼ tsp. paprika
⅛ tsp. kosher salt
⅛ tsp. coarse black pepper
12-15 sm. carrots with stems, for dipping

Whisk sour cream, mayonnaise and seasonings together in a small bowl. Cover and refrigerate for 2-3 hours before serving. Leave stems on small carrots. Clean and serve with the Herb Vegetable Dip.

Garden Fresh Scrambled Eggs ⚜

1 red bell pepper
1 yellow bell pepper
1 c. sugar snap peas
1 tsp. butter
12 eggs
1/3 c. heavy whipping cream
1/4 tsp. garlic pepper
8 oz. block jalapeño Jack cheese

Rinse, seed and dice bell peppers. Clean and cut sugar snap peas into 1/2-inch slices. Melt butter in frying pan and sauté peppers and peas for 2 minutes; remove and set aside in a bowl.

Whisk eggs in a separate bowl and fold in cream and garlic pepper. Pour egg mixture into frying pan and scramble while cooking. Cook until firm, about 3 to 5 minutes. Cut jalapeño cheese into small chunks. Fold cheese, peppers and peas into the scrambled eggs. Serve immediately.

Crepes

2 eggs	1 c. flour	2 tbsp. butter, melted
1 ¼ c. milk	1 tbsp. sugar	¼ tsp. kosher salt

Combine all ingredients together in a blender or mix in a large bowl with an electric mixer; blend well. Cover batter and chill in the refrigerator for at least 1 hour.

When ready to make the crepes, heat an electric crepe maker or a crepe pan on the stove. (A 7 ½-inch electric crepe maker was used for the small crepes. A 13-inch crepe pan with a T-shaped wooden crepe spreader was used for the large crepes.)

Once hot, dip electric crepe maker gently into the batter or scoop ¼ to ½ cup batter and pour onto the crepe pan. Spread with a T-shaped wooden spreader. For the small crepes, the indicator light shows when to remove cooked crepes. For the large crepes, turn over with spatula and cook both sides for 1 to 3 minutes. Stack or fold cooked crepes into thirds and then into thirds again (as pictured). Serve with a variety of toppings.

Chocolate Sauce ⚜

½ c. butter
2 ½ sq. unsweetened baking chocolate
1 12 oz. can evaporated milk

3 c. powdered sugar
1 ½ tsp. pure vanilla extract

In a large pot, melt butter and chocolate over low heat. Add milk and powdered sugar, stirring constantly until it comes to a boil. Reduce heat and simmer for 12 to 15 minutes. Fold in vanilla and stir. Let cool slightly before serving. Serve with small or large crepes.

Almond Whipped Cream ⚜

2 c. heavy whipping cream

⅓ – ½ c. sugar, to taste

½ tsp. pure vanilla extract

½ tsp. almond extract

Chill a metal bowl in the freezer. Remove chilled bowl and beat whipping cream with an electric mixer until stiff peaks appear. Fold in sugar, vanilla and almond extract into whipped cream; beat until stiff.

Springtime Strawberry Sauce ⚜

5 c. strawberries, divided   ¼ c. water
1 c. sugar

Rinse, remove stems and slice strawberries. Combine 3 cups sliced strawberries, sugar and water together in a saucepan. Cook over medium heat for 15 minutes or until desired thickness. Fold in remaining strawberries and place in a serving dish. Serve with crepes and whipped cream.

Cheddar Garlic Potatoes ⚜

5 lbs. russet potatoes
2 ½ tsp. kosher salt, divided
4 green onions, sliced
1 ½ c. sour cream

1 tsp. coarse black pepper
1 tsp. Italian spice seasoning
2 tsp. garlic pepper
4 c. sharp cheddar cheese, shredded

Preheat oven to 400°. Peel and dice potatoes; cook in boiling water with 1 ½ teaspoon salt for 4 to 6 minutes. Slice green onions. In a bowl, combine sour cream, pepper, remaining salt, Italian spices, garlic pepper, shredded cheese and green onions together and blend well.

Drain water from potatoes and fold in sour cream mixture. Prepare a 9 x 13 baking dish with cooking spray. Place the potato mixture in dish. Bake for 45 to 50 minutes or until brown around edges.

Savory Chicken Artichoke Sauce ⚜

1 lb. frozen chicken tenders	1 tbsp. flour	⅛ tsp. coarse black pepper
¾ c. milk	1 6 oz. jar marinated artichoke hearts	fresh parsley, for garnish
1 tbsp. butter	½ c. grated Gruyere cheese	

Spray medium stockpot with cooking spray and place over medium heat. Place frozen chicken tenders in pot and cover with a lid. Cook, stirring occasionally until the chicken is completely cooked, about 10 to 12 minutes. Remove from heat and set aside. Melt butter in a saucepan over medium heat. Whisk, while slowly adding flour to butter. Cook 1 minute until a crumbly roux forms. Gradually whisk in milk, stirring constantly. Cook 3 to 5 minutes or until thick and bubbly. Remove from heat; fold in artichoke hearts, Gruyere cheese and pepper. Using forks, pull apart cooked chicken tenders into small pieces and fold into sauce. Serve over crepes. Garnish with fresh parsley.

Asparagus Bacon Crepes ⚜

2 bundles of asparagus   1 lb. precooked bacon

Preheat oven to 400°. Rinse and remove bottom 2 inches of asparagus spears and discard. Blanch asparagus in boiling water for 2 minutes. Drain and place in a serving dish. Place precooked bacon on a jelly roll pan and cook in oven for 4 minutes or until desired crispness. Cut bacon into small pieces and transfer to serving dish with asparagus. Fill crepes with asparagus and bacon. Pour Gruyere Cheese Sauce over crepes and garnish with crisp bacon.

Ham & Swiss Crepes ⚜

1 ½ lb. honey cured ham
2 tbsp. butter

1 ½ lb. block Swiss cheese
fresh parsley, for garnish

Cut ham into small cubes. Melt butter in frying pan and sauté ham over medium-high heat, until edges brown. Cut swiss cheese into small cubes. Toss with fried ham and place in serving dish. Fill crepes with ham and Swiss cheese cubes. Pour hot Gruyere Cheese Sauce over crepes and top with fresh parsley.

Gruyere Cheese Sauce ⚜

3/4 c. milk
1 tbsp. butter

1 tbsp. flour
1/2 c. grated Gruyere cheese

1/4 tsp. kosher salt
1/8 tsp. coarse black pepper

Warm the milk in a small saucepan. Melt butter in another saucepan over medium heat. Whisk, while slowly adding flour to butter. Cook 1 minute until a crumbly roux forms. Gradually whisk in warm milk, stirring constantly. Cook 3 to 5 minutes or until thick and bubbly. Remove from heat; whisk in cheese, salt and pepper.

Cinnamon Oatmeal Pound Cake ⚜

1 c. butter, softened
2 c. sugar
½ tsp. kosher salt
2 tsp. ground cinnamon
3 eggs, whisked
1 tsp. pure vanilla extract
¾ c. sour cream
2 ½ c. flour
2 tsp. baking powder

Crumble:
    1 ½ c. brown sugar
    ¾ c. flour
    1 tsp. ground cinnamon
    ½ tsp. kosher salt
    ½ c. butter, softened
    2 c. rolled oats

Preheat oven to 350°. Prepare a round bundt pan with cooking spray. In a mixing bowl, with an electric mixer, beat together the butter, sugar, salt and cinnamon until blended and fluffy. Add eggs and beat. Stir in vanilla and sour cream, mixing thoroughly. In a separate bowl, whisk flour and baking powder; add to wet ingredients and mix well. Make Crumble, by combining brown sugar, flour, cinnamon and salt together. Cut in butter with a pastry cutter and add the rolled oats. Set aside.

Fold in half of the Crumble mixture into the batter and gently stir but do not over blend. Pour batter into prepared pan and top with remaining crumble. Bake for 35 to 45 minutes or until toothpick inserted in the center comes out clean. Drizzle Brown Butter Frosting over the top of the pound cake. Slice cake and serve.

Brown Butter Frosting ⚜

½ c. butter   2-3 c. powdered sugar   1 tsp. pure vanilla extract

Melt butter, over medium heat in a small saucepan and cook until butter is golden brown, about 2 to 3 minutes. Remove from heat and stir in 2 cups powdered sugar and vanilla. If thicker frosting is desired add more powdered sugar. Drizzle Brown Butter Frosting over the top of the Cinnamon Oatmeal Pound Cake. Slice cake and serve.

Oatmeal Raisin Pecan Cookies ⚜

3 eggs
1 c. raisins
1 tsp. pure vanilla extract
1 c. butter, softened
1 c. brown sugar

1 c. sugar
2 ½ c. flour
1 tsp. kosher salt
1 tsp. ground cinnamon

1 tsp. ground nutmeg
2 tsp. baking soda
2 c. rolled oats
¾ c. chopped pecans

Beat eggs in a small mixing bowl. Add raisins and vanilla. Let stand 1 hour. Preheat oven to 350°. In a separate mixing bowl, cream butter and sugars with an electric mixer. Whisk together flour, salt, cinnamon, nutmeg, baking soda and rolled oats; add to butter mixture and blend well. Stir in egg and raisin mixture. Fold in pecans. Drop dough by heaping teaspoons onto ungreased jelly roll pan. Bake for 10 to12 minutes or until lightly browned. Do not overbake.

Details...

We used a large candle encircled by a robin's blue egg wreath as the centerpiece for this blissful morning brunch. Smaller candles are arranged in glass pedestal containers surrounded by small pastel chocolate robin eggs. Votive candles placed in colorful egg cups line the tablescape.

Notes & Comments

Shopping List

Each recipe is designed to serve ten to twelve

2 lbs. thick sliced, oven roasted deli turkey

1 ½ lbs. honey cured ham

1 lb. frozen chicken tenders

1 lb. precooked bacon

8 oz. block jalapeño Jack cheese

4 c. sharp cheddar cheese

1 ½ lb. block Swiss cheese

1 c. grated Gruyere cheese

2 doz. + 4 eggs

1 lb. butter

2 ⅓ c. heavy whipping cream

2 ¾ c. sour cream

2 lemons

1 c. blueberries

6 c. strawberries

1 c. cantaloupe

1 c. pineapple

1 c. grapes

1 c. raspberries

1 c. honeydew melon

10 tangerines

1 tbsp. fresh chopped chives

15 sm. carrots with stems

1 red bell pepper

1 yellow bell pepper

1 c. sugar snap peas

2 heads hearts of romaine

3 avocados

3 tomatoes

1 lime

5 lbs. russet potatoes

4 green onions

1 bundle fresh parsley

2 bundles of asparagus

Shopping List

Each recipe is designed to serve ten to twelve

1 tsp. dill weed
1 tsp. dried tarragon leaves
1 tbsp. parsley flakes
¼ tsp. paprika
2 ¼ tsp. garlic pepper
½ tsp. almond extract
½ tsp. dried oregano
½ tsp. dried basil

1 tsp. Italian spice seasoning
1 c. rice vinegar
1 6 oz. jar marinated artichoke hearts
¾ c. chopped pecans
2 ½ sq. unsweetened baking chocolate
1 12 oz. can evaporated milk
4 c. rolled oats
1 c. raisins

Staples:

flour	pure vanilla extract	vegetable oil
baking powder	sugar	kosher salt
baking soda	powdered sugar	onion salt
ground cinnamon	brown sugar	coarse black pepper
ground nutmeg	milk	mayonnaise

shopping lists available for print online.

❧ Index ❧

Shrimp Avocado Salad.............................185
Shrimp Endive Boats.............................151
Shrimp Zucchini Quiche.........................94

Fruits

Apple Orchard Crisp.............................56
Apple Pomegranate Salad......................107
Bavarian Apple Torte.............................74
Citrus Glazed Fruit Salad......................200
Ghosts of Halloween Past......................40
Old Glory Fruit Tray.............................12
Pear & Gorgonzola Endive Boats............151
Pomegranate Orange Salad....................146
Sugar Cookie Fruit Pizzas.....................162

Main Dishes & Meats

Bacon Wrapped Turkey Tenderloins............54
Beef Wellington.................................110
Cauldron Baked Lasagna........................32
Cilantro Fish Tacos.............................154
Classic Quiche Lorraine........................88
Easter Egg Cobb Salad.........................201
Green Chili Soup.................................157
Ham & Swiss Crepes.............................212
Italian Basil Quiche..............................90
Lemon Pepper Chicken Strips.................189
Orange Shrimp Pasta Salad....................28
Oven Roasted French Onion Soup.............97
Picnic Pulled Pork...............................16
Potato Crusted Jalapeño Quiche.............92
Ribeye Tostadas.................................152
Rosemary Chicken...............................72
Savory Chicken Artichoke Sauce.............210
Shrimp Avocado Salad.........................185
Shrimp Zucchini Quiche........................94
Split Pea Soup...................................70
Steak & Gorgonzola Salad.....................170
Veggie Quiche...................................86
Wicked Good Mac & Cheese....................31
Winter White Cauliflower Soup................173
Witch's Chili Brew...............................35

Pasta

Cauldron Baked Lasagna........................32
Orange Shrimp Pasta Salad....................28
Star Studded Pasta Salad......................15
Wicked Good Mac & Cheese....................31

Pies, Tarts & Tortes

Autumn Ice Cream Pie..........................39
Bavarian Apple Torte...........................74
Chocolate Almond Tortes.....................133
Lemon Cheesecake Tartlets...................176
Sugar Cookie Fruit Pizzas.....................162
Thanksgiving Pecan Pie........................57

Quiches

Classic Quiche Lorraine........................88
Italian Basil Quiche..............................90
Potato Crusted Jalapeño Quiche.............92
Shrimp Zucchini Quiche........................94
Veggie Quiche...................................86

Salad Dressings

Balsamic Vinaigrette Dressing................143
Black Poppy Seed Dressing....................28
Champagne Vinaigrette Dressing.............147
Cobb Dressing..................................201
Creamy Garlic Pepper Dressing...............13
Creamy Italian Dressing........................14
Ginger Rice Vinegar Dressing.................142
Grey Poupon Dressing.........................171
Italian Vinaigrette..............................185
Red Wine Vinaigrette...........................67
Red Wine Vinegar Dressing...................140
Spicy Ranch Dressing..........................141
Sweet Pomegranate Dressing................107

Salads

Sauces & Syrups

Side Dishes

Soups

Vegetables

✦ Acknowledgements ✦

Thanks to our very talented graphic designer Brayden Iwasaki for long hours of hard work. A special thanks to our gifted photographer Suzy Oliveira who never ceases to amaze us.

A special thanks to those who shared their unique gifts and talents:

Rachael Crittenden
Maggie Fish
Shauna Benne
Carolyn Kirkham Greene
Bonnie Clark
Marianne LeSueur
Tammy Neslen
Beth Lindorf
Karen Nelson
Ellen Leake
Gretel Swensen
Dana Johnson
Denise Fielding
Brynlee Fielding Kunz
Eli Clarke
Susan Gillenwater

A special thanks to
Tina Alcivar for a great job of peeling,
chopping and making things fun.

A big hug to my little angels
Grace and Chloé Huxtable
for helping with the dishes

Thanks to our gracious editors:
Jean Olsen
Jocelyn Juran

Location Credits:
Rick and Christena Durham
Paul and Kelly Harris
Bryan and Bronte Clarke
Larry and Cory Maxfield

A special thank you to

www.4-chairs.com

Thanksgiving, New Year's Eve
and Valentine's Chapters

*M*ichelle Huxtable has successfully created gathering places for many years as an interior designer. Her passion for creating a comfortable and inviting atmosphere is motivated by her innate desire to surround herself and others with beauty. She derives great joy from gathering her family and friends around the table. She feels that food is a love language and that lovingly preparing a meal is a genuine expression of oneself. Michelle has owned an interior design firm for over 20 years. She also enjoys working with her husband in the construction industry. This is her sixth book in *The Gathering of Friends* cookbook series. She has six children, one daughter-in-law, three sons-in-law and twelve wonderful grandchildren.

*A*bby Jane Green studied in New York and London before graduating from Brigham Young University in Art History and Curatorial Studies. She is a gifted artist and has enjoyed contributing to *The Gathering of Friends* cookbook series. She is Michelle Huxtable's oldest daughter and loves to work with her mother. She and her husband Tyson enjoy cooking together and creating Italian recipes. They reside in Salt Lake City, Utah. Their home has been graced by the birth of their son Everett, with a little brother soon to arrive.